HINDU
GODS & GODDESSES

by Prem P. Bhalla

A glimpse into their vibrant world

HINDOOLOGY
BOOKS

Published by

HINDOOLOGY
BOOKS

An imprint of
Pustak Mahal®, Delhi

J-3/16, Daryaganj, New Delhi-110002
☎ 23276539, 23272783, 23272784 • *Fax:* 011-23260518
E-mail: info@pustakmahal.com • *Website:* www.pustakmahal.com

London Office
5, Roddell Court, Bath Road, Slough SL3 OQJ, England
E-mail: pustakmahaluk@pustakmahal.com

Sales Centres
10-B, Netaji Subhash Marg, Daryaganj, New Delhi-110002
☎ 23268292, 23268293, 23279900 • *Fax:* 011-23280567
E-mail: rapidexdelhi@indiatimes.com

Branch Offices
Bangalore: ☎ 22234025
E-mail: pmblr@sancharnet.in • pustak@sancharnet.in
Mumbai: ☎ 22010941
E-mail: rapidex@bom5.vsnl.net.in
Patna: ☎ 3294193 • *Telefax:* 0612-2302719
E-mail: rapidexptn@rediffmail.com
Hyderabad: *Telefax:* 040-24737290
E-mail: pustakmahalhyd@yahoo.co.in

© Copyright : Hindoology Books
ISBN 978-81-223-0969-0

Edition : April 2007

Designed by : **Ritu Sinha**
Photographic Credits : Snehaunshuchowdhury, A. Carvin, Bhansingh, Mysore Ashrama,
Guru Mustak Singh, Sundar, Shivamohan, Andrea Aditi

Printed at : Gopsons Papers Ltd., Noida.

Dedicated to the
Eager Devotee
in search of the Perfect God

CONTENTS

Preface

No major religion in the world can claim to have as many gods and goddesses as Hinduism. At the same time, no other religion has as many forms of worship and places of pilgrimage as do the Hindus.

The plurality of gods and goddesses are not evidence of different streams of thought, neither are they there to create confusion: they fulfil a definite purpose. Each god and goddess is assigned a special responsibility. In their own sphere of activity, they are benevolent. One would normally expect the gods and goddesses to be perfect in every way. But they are not. They are perfect in their sphere of activity only. In this respect, they are human. They make mistakes, are punished for them, and then amend their ways. This makes them easier to understand and to relate to.

This study on Hindu gods and goddesses is aimed at enabling an average person to better understand the Hindu religious ideology, and thereby live a better life, find greater fulfilment and gradually rise spiritually. A contented person is always happy. An attempt has been made to take a wide view that would fulfil the aspirations of all sections of society. Hinduism is a very old religion. It has withstood the onslaughts of a variety of political upheavals and rulers who were brought up with different religious thought and background.

Even within Hindu thought, the thinking of Bhagwan Mahavir renewed attention towards Jainism; the thinking of Gautam Buddha gave birth to Buddhism, a system of thought that found greater acceptance outside rather than within India. More recently, the coming of Guru Nanak brought significant changes. With a call for simplification of rites and rituals, the modern society that thinks more globally than locally searches for answers to their questions pertaining to spiritual growth. They search for a god or goddess who delivers; one who can dispel their doubts about everyday things.

Much of the information in this book has been derived from the Hindu religious texts. Since a lot of earlier pre-historic information was passed orally from one generation to another, and was recorded much later, there might be variations between one version and another. However, the basic concepts that are explained remain the same.

Whatever different people may say, there is no doubt that there is only one Super Being, or Cosmic Energy, that controls the universe. The many gods and goddesses are manifestations of this Super Being to fulfil different tasks. The questioning person needs to understand the background of the gods and goddesses, and also how they influence the common man. Once this is done, it becomes easier to give shape to individual spiritual aspirations and thoughts.

I am particularly grateful to Shri R.A. Gupta, Managing Director, and Shri S.K. Roy, Executive Editor, Pustak Mahal Publishers, for permission to draw some references from their publications.

—*Prem P. Bhalla*

1

Prologue

PROLOGUE

Do Hindus really have myriad gods and goddesses? Given their different attributes, don't the many gods and goddesses create confusion in the minds of devotees? Which god or goddess can help the devotee achieve greater success? And sooner? Which god or goddess is easier to please than the others? Is it not difficult to choose one god from another? Does this not make Hinduism a unique religion?

To answer these questions, we must first know whom we accept as a god or goddess. As commonly accepted, God is the creator and supreme ruler of the universe, often referred to as the Supreme Being. However, we also accept anyone possessing some of the attributes of the Supreme Being as a god or goddess. An object or being that is benevolent like the Supreme Being immediately attracts adoration and reverence, and may become worthy of worship. This attribute by itself makes it easier to understand the concept of many gods and goddesses.

Just as attributes of compassion and benevolence are honoured and worshipped, objects and beings that inspire awe and fear are dreaded. The object of life is peaceful existence. To escape harm, one respects these attributes of brute strength and terror with equal fervour.

Both gods and demons are creations of the human mind. While gods emerge from — and thrive upon — positive values like patience, tolerance, love and forgiveness, demons show up as greed, anger, jealousy, attachment, lust and pride. While gods lead one to a path of truth,

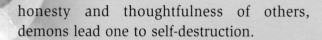

honesty and thoughtfulness of others, demons lead one to self-destruction.

A Hindu is a person who adheres to Hinduism — a religion followed by the vast majority in India. Hinduism is the oldest of all religions. It is more about what people do than what they think. It is liberal in its outlook. It permits everyone to follow a way of life that is meaningful to the individual. No individual or prophet founded it. While the origins of other religions can be dated fairly accurately, Hinduism emerges from the mists of time. It is a synthesis of a variety of religious experiences, and offers a complete view of life. It is tolerant of how individuals interpret it in their own life. Hinduism continues to be a practical philosophy of life. It is amidst such a background that we come across the many Hindu gods and goddesses.

Hindus follow a way of life founded upon the teachings in the four **Vedas** — the **Rig-Veda,** the **Yajur-Veda,** the **Sama-Veda** and the **Atharva-Veda.** The Vedas do not belong to any particular time or place. They pertain to mankind and provide knowledge about every aspect of life — the study of phonetics, the code of rituals, grammar, etymology, literature, astronomy, archery, music and architecture.

The Upanishads — ancient Sanskrit religious scriptures — follow the revelations of the Vedas. Since they come at the end of the Vedas, they are also referred to as

Vedanta (*Veda-anta,* meaning *end of knowledge.* The word upa-ni-shad (meaning *sit down near*) suggests a personal touch to explaining a religious truth. Almost 200 Upanishads add to the knowledge provided by the four Vedas. These emphasize the existence of the soul, its immortality, and of rebirth based upon an individual's actions, or karma.

The epics, **Ramayan** and **Mahabharat,** followed the Upanishads. Both are narrated as meaningful classics containing stories, tales and discourses about life and living. They date back to over 2000 years, but are popular and meaningful in the context of modern life. They have been converted to films and television serials. They have provided inspiration and direction to millions of people, and will continue to do so for all time.

The **Puranas** were composed after the epics. They describe in detail many of the subjects and the characters in the epics, and also describe the virtues and failings of the myriad Hindu gods and goddesses. The Puranas elaborate on the hymns of praise, philosophies and rituals. They cover five distinct subjects — the creation of the universe; its destruction and regeneration; the genealogy of gods and patriarchs; the reigns of the Manus, and the history of the solar and lunar races of kings. There are 18 Puranas, grouped in three divisions pertaining to Brahma, Vishnu and Shiva. In addition, there are 18 Up-puranas.

The **Dharmashastras** and **Dharmasutras** (textbooks on sacred law) provide guidelines on the Hindu way of life and living. Dharmashastra is a term applicable to the laws of Manu, Yagyavalkya and other sages who first recorded the **Smritis.** An important Dharmasutra is the work of the sage Jaimini, a disciple of Vyas; it is on law and customs.

Most of the details contained in this book have been derived from these valuable texts.

The Supreme Being

2

THE SUPREME BEING

The creator and the sustainer of the universe is accepted as the Supreme Being, or God. Different people have varied perceptions of what God looks like. One visualizes and prays in whatever form one prefers to see Him. It is believed that God is eternal. He has no beginning and no end. He has no form. He is a being of light, a tiny spark, a storehouse of eternal energy. He is **Brahman** to Hindus.

Does this description not liken God to the sun? It is true that the sun provides light and energy. However, if God has created the entire cosmos, and the sun is only a part of the whole creation, how can God be what He has created and sustains? His attributes are undoubtedly beyond all limits.

In the **Swateshwar Upanishad**, it is said:
There is one God. He resides within everyone. He is universal. He is present as the soul in every living being.

In the **Bhagavad Gita**, 13/13, it is said:
God is everywhere. He can touch and feel everything. He can see everywhere. He can hear everything. There is no place without Him. He can understand everything. There is nothing that He cannot see. There is nothing that He cannot accept. He can reach everywhere.

Again, in the **Bhagavad Gita**, 13/15, it is said:
The true supreme spirit resides within the body and the mind. However, it is so subtle that it cannot be perceived by the senses. It is close at hand, and yet far away.

In the **Yajur-Veda**, 40/1, it is said:
In this world God resides in all things.

In the **Mundak**, 2/2/11, it is said:
Like the nectar of immortality, the eternal spirit faces you. It is behind you. It is on your right and to your left side. It is below you. It is above you. The entire cosmos is filled with the universal spirit of God.

If the Supreme Being is within each one of us, why can we not see or feel Him? Why can we not feel and enjoy the happiness, peace and bliss that are attributes of God? We fail to enjoy the many attributes of God as, due to degeneration over several births, we have overlooked the presence of God within us. Just as we cannot see our image in a mirror covered with dust, we cannot see God within us because the virtues are hidden by ignorance. Negative attributes like greed, anger, jealousy, hypocrisy and pride, that are like demons, prevent us from meeting the God within.

In the **Narad Purana**, Purvkhand, 11/57-64, it is said that people who give up attachment, maliciousness and hypocrisy can experience the God within. Similarly, those who are free of greed and jealousy, are honest and sincere, respect their parents, teachers and elders, are kind and hospitable to guests, live in the company of good people, go on pilgrimage, and offer food and charity will always find God within them.

To experience God, one needs to be pure and virtuous. As we have seen, one fails to remain pure and virtuous because of slow degeneration over past births. To regain purity, one needs to shed negative attributes and develop latent virtues. This is possible when the soul takes control of the physical body. This is not easy because while the soul directs the body in one

direction, the body pulls the soul to the easier and pleasurable path where the senses enjoy the world around them.

It is equally significant that God has given every individual the freedom of thought and action. It is a personal choice whether one accepts the more difficult path of virtue, or follows the vast majority on the path of pleasure and enjoyment. It is this choice that can either raise humanity to divinity, or drag it down to gross depravity, suffering and pain. We notice a cyclic action not only in the lives of individuals but also in the environment and humanity when we see that the golden era degenerates to the silver, copper and iron eras to be followed once again by the golden era.

What happens when humanity degenerates to the level of no return, and there is universal suffering?

Sri Krishna answers this question in the **Bhagavad Gita**, 4/7-8:
O people of Bharat, whenever there is degeneration of thought and increase in sin, I shall incarnate in different forms... I will protect and support honest and virtuous people, and destroy those who live in sin. I shall incarnate era after era to establish righteousness.

Since God has no form, to protect the righteous and the virtuous, God has emerged in the world in many forms to guide and teach humanity to live an ideal life. Individuals believe and follow whatever they can comprehend personally, or through experience handed down to them by others. This explains the emergence and acceptance of many gods and goddesses, who ended suffering and became dear to their devotees.

3

Sri Ganesh

SRI GANESH

Sri Ganeshaya Nama! The elder of the two sons of Shiva and Parvati, Sri Ganesh, the elephant-headed god, is recognised as the Supreme Leader **(Vinayaka)**, the Lord who overcomes all obstacles **(Vighaneshwar)** and as the Leader of *Ganas* **(Ganpati)**. Both, Saraswati, the Goddess of Knowledge, and Lakshmi, the Goddess of Wealth and Prosperity, favour him to make him the master of knowledge, success and achievement.

Sri Ganesh is the most revered of Hindu gods. He is so blessed that before any ceremony or auspicious occasion, prayers must first be offered to him. He is *vighnaharta* and master of Riddhi-Siddhi. This simply means that he removes all obstacles that confront devotees. A prayer, an offering or penance made for him ensures success, wealth and prosperity.

The elephant head is not without significance. The fan-like ears make Sri Ganesh a keen listener, one who comprehends knowledge well. The sharp eyes make him an eager observer. Together, the eyes and the ears contribute to make him wise and learned. They also add to his ability to discriminate between good and evil. The trunk is unique in that it can not only smell, but is equally capable of picking up something as small as a blade of grass, or a huge object like a tree trunk. While the two tusks represent the power to discern between good and evil, the broken tusk is symbolic that Sri Ganesh is above the pairs of opposites like joy and sorrow that affect mankind. The wide mouth enables Sri Ganesh to eat enough to humble the pride of Kuber, God of Wealth. Yet it can be satisfied with a few blades of *durva* grass or a *modak* offered with devotion. The potbelly is large enough to accommodate all kinds of experiences.

Sri Ganesh has four hands. He carries a rope in one hand and an axe in another. He holds a modak in one hand and blesses the devotees with the other. While the axe is symbolic of severing the devotee's attachment with worldly things, the rope is used to pull him closer to the truth. The modak is symbolic of the fruit of devotion. The blessings ensure success to all devotees.

Sri Ganesh has a mouse for a vehicle. A mouse is small but left by itself it can cause great havoc. However, in the control of Sri Ganesh it has the ability to carry its master to the most difficult of places.

Birth of Sri Ganesh

There has always been a struggle between good and evil. When in distress, the only option available to the good is to seek the support of the gods who could suppress evil.

The **Linga Purana** describes the birth of Sri Ganesh. The gods, led by their guru, Brihaspati, at one time approached Shiva to protect them from the demons, who were destroying everything that the gods did. Ready to help them, Shiva glanced at Parvati, and a baby boy with an elephant-like head manifested. The gods were overjoyed at the sight as Parvati dressed up the child with the best of clothes and jewellery. Shiva picked up the child and said, "You have taken birth to fulfil the desires of the gods, and to destroy the evil demons. Even those who seek to have their desires fulfilled through devotion to Brahma, Vishnu or me must first seek your grace via prayer and worship. Without your favour, they will fail."

In the **Padma Purana,** it is explained that after their marriage Shiva and Parvati lived together, moving through beautiful gardens and lonely forests. Deeply attached to Lord Shiva, while bathing, Parvati created a male form with an elephant-like head in great ecstasy. As she dipped the male form into the holy river Ganga, it came alive. Parvati called him 'son'. The gods rejoiced to see the child with spiritual glory. They called him "**Gangeya**", meaning the son of Ganga. Lord Brahma made him the leader of the **Ganas** — Shiva's attendants, and he came to be known as Ganpati.

The **Shiva Purana** has a similar but more detailed explanation of Sri Ganesh's birth. Once Parvati's personal lady attendants told her that the Ganas who stood guard at Kailash were more devoted to Lord Shiva than to her. Since there were many visitors to Kailash, it would be wise to have Ganas that were completely loyal to her. She heard the suggestion, but paid no heed.

One day when Parvati went for a bath, she posted Shiva's favourite Gana, Nandi, to stand guard outside. When Shiva came, Nandi asked him to wait until Parvati came out. Shiva paid no heed and walked in, much to Parvati's embarrassment. Then Parvati recalled her attendant's suggestion.

The next time before a bath, Parvati created a baby boy and, as a son, ordered him to stand guard where she bathed. When Shiva came, the little boy refused him permission to enter. An argument ensued. When Shiva summoned other Ganas, the little boy emphasized that he was Parvati's attendant, and would not permit anyone to enter. Interpreting the boy's devotion as audacity, Shiva lost his temper. In anger, he cut off the boy's head with his trident.

When Parvati emerged from her bath and saw her son without a head, her rage knew no bounds. She smashed everything around her. Fear struck everyone. Shiva and the others tried to pacify her, to no avail. Repentant, at his error, Shiva sent out his attendants to cut off the head of the first living being they came across. They found a baby elephant. Cutting off the head they brought it to Shiva, who joined it to the body. Thus was Sri Ganesh born. Shiva and Parvati delightedly picked up the little boy.

In the **Brahmavaivarta Purana** there is another explanation of Sri Ganesh's birth. After their marriage, Shiva and Parvati were together for a long time enjoying great bliss. One day, Parvati expressed a desire to Lord Shiva that she desired a noble son. Lord Shiva was in agreement, but suggested that to have a truly noble son she needed to observe a *vrata*, or vow, known as Punyaka, for a full year. She expressed her willingness and a day was fixed for the commencement of the vow. Gods and goddesses visited Mt. Kailash to offer greetings and good wishes. Lord Vishnu personally blessed Parvati. The celestial sage, Sanatkumar, offered that he could serve as the priest for the yearlong prayers.

When the year ended, and it was time to conclude the ceremony with *dakshina*, or reward, to the priest, Sanatkumar demanded that Lord Shiva be given to him as dakshina. Parvati could not believe such an impossible demand. She offered a variety of articles, but Sanatkumar was insistent. He wanted Lord Shiva, or nothing. Parvati feared that if Sanatkumar did not accept dakshina, the yearlong prayer would be worth nothing. Parvati was at a loss how to handle the situation, and went to Vishnu, who suggested that she should give away Shiva, and later exchange him by offering a hundred thousand cows. She did that and concluded the fast. But when she offered a hundred thousand cows to Sanatkumar in exchange for Shiva, he said that he had no use for the cows. He refused to let Shiva go back.

Parvati felt devastated. She had lost her Lord forever. How could she live without him? Her desire for a son had ruined her. It was best that she ended her life. She closed her eyes to pray to Sri Krishna, who appeared to rid her of all her sorrows. As the gods and goddesses saw the divine forms of Sri Krishna and Parvati, they went to Sanatkumar to persuade him to send back Shiva to Parvati. He readily agreed. Lord Shiva was back with Parvati.

Lord Shiva and Parvati together organized a great feast, honouring everyone who attended the ceremony. Amidst

the great crowd, a weak old Brahmin appeared and begged for food. He said he was famished. Shiva and Parvati stepped forward and asked him what he desired. The Brahmin said that he desired to taste and eat the many kinds of food. He wanted to eat till his appetite was satiated and he became potbellied. He desired that he might be clothed with rich robes and ornaments, be seated on a throne and taught the sacred *mantras* that would make him an ardent devotee of the Supreme Being. He continued further to say — what was there that a mother could not provide to her son?

Parvati was moved to hear the Brahmin, but before she could do anything he was gone. She looked around with disappointment. Just then there was a celestial call: "Mother, go to your room. Your son awaits you." Parvati rushed to her room to find a charming son lying on her bed. Parvati picked him up with great joy. Mount Kailash resounded with music and dance. The gods and goddesses greeted the little boy and the parents.

As Parvati sat on the bed with the baby boy she noticed that amongst the many visitors Shani (Saturn) stood aside with his head turned away. He offered his greetings but would not look at Parvati, or the baby boy. When asked why he was averting his gaze from her and the baby, he said that he was compelled to do so because he did not want to cause her any misery. There was a curse on him by his wife that whoever he would gaze at, would have their head cut off. Parvati heard him but disagreed because the world moved at the will of the Lord. On her insistence Shani looked at the baby, and lo! The boy's head was cut off!

Parvati could not believe what she saw. She fainted with grief. A great commotion overtook Mt. Kailash. Vishnu reached there in all haste. He cut off the head of a baby elephant and grafted it on the baby's body. With his blessings, the baby came alive again. He performed the rituals in the presence of the gods, goddesses, saints and others present. He gave the child eight names: **Vighanesh**, **Ganesh**, **Heramba**, **Gajanana**, **Lambodara**, **Ekadanta**, **Soorpakarna** and **Vinayaka**. Then he said, "I am the first to honour and worship you. You deserve to be offered the first prayer and worship by whoever conducts a ritual or a ceremony."

Incarnations of Sri Ganesh

In the **Ganesh Purana** it is explained that Sri Ganesh incarnated in all the four eras to overcome demoniac forces. In the Satyayug, he incarnated as **Mahotkata Vinayaka** and overcame the demons Narantaka and Devantaka. In Tretayug, **Sri Ganesh** appeared as **Sri Mayuresh** and overcame Sindhu. In Dwaparyug, he appeared as Sri Gajanana and destroyed Sindur. In Kaliyug, he appeared as **Sri Dhoomraketu** to destroy innumerable demons.

In the **Mudgala Purana** it is explained that Sri Ganesh incarnated on eight different occasions as **Vakratunda**, **Ekadanta**, **Mahodara**, **Gajanana**, **Lambodara**, **Vikata**, **Vighanraja** and as **Dhooravarna.** The enemies that these incarnations overcame were none other than the enemies an average person faces in everyday life — lust, anger, greed, attachment, pride and arrogance. The saints and sages at that time described through stories how one could overcome human frailties through discipline and a virtuous life. It is no different today. The devotees still seek the blessings of Sri Ganesh to live a life free of evil and sin.

Wisdom of Sri Ganesh

There are many stories in the Puranas and the Up-puranas about Sri Ganesh's wisdom. He had a younger brother named Kartikeya, who moved to South India when Sri Ganesh convinced the parents that he must be married first.

The stories repeatedly emphasize Sri Ganesh's devotion to his parents. He loves to eat. This explains his potbelly. But he is equally easy to please with a few blades of durva grass or a modak offered with sincerity and devotion. This makes him the god of the masses. He helps them get over their obstacles and achieve success. With his wisdom he is quick to see insincerity and pride.

He is equally swift in punishing the proud. Even as a child he humbled Kuber, the God of Wealth, who wanted to show off his prosperity to Shiva. As a young boy he confronted

Parasuram, Shiva's ardent devotee, when he insisted upon entering the gateway leading to Shiva's personal chambers. In the same way he humbled Tulsi who desired to marry him, but he refused. He did not hesitate to curse and humble Chandrama (the moon) who laughed at him for falling off his vehicle — a mouse.

When Ved Vyas decided to compose the epic **Mahabharat**, he went to Brahma seeking his help in locating a person who could take dictation. Brahma said that there could be no better person than Sri Ganesh to do the needful. Sri Ganesh agreed, but imposed the condition that he would take dictation and write only as long as the dictation was uninterrupted. That was a difficult suggestion to accept, but not to offend a wise person, he put in the counter condition that Sri Ganesh would write only after he had comprehended what was being dictated. That would give Ved Vyas the time to think and dictate new verses. The complete understanding of the wisdom of the Mahabharat and the Bhagavad Gita that forms a part of it, only made Sri Ganesh wiser.

Worship to Sri Ganesh

Thousands of years after the Vedas, Upanishads and Puranas were composed, Sri Ganesh continues to be the God of the masses. Millions of Hindus pray to him every day to get rid of the obstacles in their way, and to seek strength and inspiration to achieve success. Innumerable temples dedicated to Sri Ganesh stand all over the country and abroad. The Siddhi Vinayaka Temple at Mumbai is one of the most popular temples where hundreds of thousands of devotees visit each year.

Blessed by both Vishnu and Shiva, and also other gods, prayers are offered to Sri Ganesh on all auspicious occasions and before all other gods. Ganesh Chaturthi is celebrated with great fervour in many parts of the country. Idols of Sri Ganesh are made and prayers offered. At the end of the prayers, the idols are immersed in rivers or the sea. During Diwali, prayers are offered to Sri Ganesh and Lakshmi. For this purpose, millions of little idols of Sri Ganesh and Lakshmi made of clay find their way into Hindu homes.

Sri Ganesh is a benevolent god ready to bless one with good health, success and happiness in return for sincere love and devotion.

4

The Hindu Trinity

THE HINDU TRINITY

Hindu religious thought is based upon three principal gods — Brahma, Vishnu and Shiva. The three support the Supreme Being, and are responsible for creating, preserving and destroying the universe.

Brahma is the first member of the Hindu Trinity. He is said to have created the universe and everything in it. He is also known as ***Prajapati***. The word *praja* means *populace* and *pati* means *master*. Together they mean *master of the populace*. It is also believed that he created ten Prajapatis who helped in creating the universe. Brahma had five heads. Shiva cut off one. The four heads are symbolic of the four Vedas, of the four *yugas* (ages or eras) and also of the four castes amongst Hindus.

Vishnu is the second god of the Hindu Trinity. He has a thousand names and several incarnations. Of these, ten hold special significance. The last one, Kalki, is yet to come.

Shiva is the third god of the Hindu Trinity. He represents both death that destroys, and reproduction that follows destruction. He destroys and disintegrates. After destruction, he helps in reproducing again. He is also known by many names. As a benevolent god, he is known as **Shankar**, **Mahadev** and **Vishwanath**. As one who destroys he is known as **Rudra**, **Mahakal**, **Virbhadra** and **Bhairav**.

If the Hindu trinity is revered, the wives are equally revered. As the creator, Brahma created **Saraswati**. He married her and, therefore, she is revered as his wife. She is the goddess of speech, learning and knowledge. Those who pursue learning hold her in high reverence and seek her blessings.

Vishnu's wife **Lakshmi** is revered as the goddess of beauty, good fortune and prosperity. She went through several incarnations to be with Vishnu. Almost every Hindu home has her image. Businessmen specially revere her.

Parvati is an incarnation of Gauri, the daughter of Daksh. She could marry Shiva only after severe penance. All Hindu women aspire to have a married life like that of Parvati. For a good partner and a happy married life, unmarried youth, particularly women, pray to Shiva and Parvati. Just as Shiva changed forms to be both benevolent and destructive, Parvati too changed forms. As the divine universal power, she is called Shakti. In her destructive form, she is Kali.

Brahma's role was that of a creator. After he created the universe and humankind, the role of preserving it was that of Vishnu. He fulfilled this role by taking several forms through incarnations. Shiva fulfils the role of destruction and regeneration.

There are many temples devoted to Vishnu and Shiva, and their many forms. But there is only one temple devoted to Brahma at Pushkar, near Ajmer in Rajasthan. It is human nature to seek what one does not have. It is easy to harbour thoughts, but difficult to sustain good thoughts and intentions. To enable us to do so, we seek the help of Vishnu. He helps us in our efforts. Similarly, it is easy to harbour negative thoughts but we cannot easily destroy them. We seek the help of Shiva to do so. We repeatedly need Vishnu and Shiva, and propitiate them through the many places of prayer. Since creation does not offer problems, we do not always seek the help of Brahma.

In everyday life, mankind seeks the favours of Vishnu and Shiva along with the three goddesses — Saraswati, Lakshmi and Parvati.

Boons by the Trinity

Each member of the Hindu Trinity fulfils special responsibilities, and are revered for their attributes and abilities. To gain from their special powers, many individuals have offered prayers and penance to seek their favours. Pleased with the devotion of these individuals, each of the three gods have been known to grant boons, most of which have been utilized positively. But there are several instances when individuals exploited the benevolence of the deity and sought boons that eventually became a nuisance for mankind.

In the **Ramayan** we read of Ravan, who sought a boon that he die neither in the day, nor at night. Kumbhkaran asked for a strange boon. He slept for six months and woke up only for a day. That single day was like hell for everyone around him. Meghnad sought a blessing that he could hide in the clouds and fight. Vali was so blessed that whoever faced him in battle lost half his strength. To end their tyranny, Vishnu incarnated as Sri Ram to kill Ravan, Kumbhkaran, and others of their kind. He also killed Vali. Lakshman killed Meghnad.

When blessings are utilized for the welfare of humankind, they grow. However, when pride takes root because of a special blessing, it gradually turns into arrogance, and becomes a misfortune for humankind. In every such instance,

Vishnu, Shiva, or one or more of the three goddesses intervened to bring the situation under control.

There is a legend that pleased with the devotion of the demon Bhasmasura, Shiva once granted him a boon that any person or object he touched would be reduced to ashes. It was a strange request, but having agreed to grant a boon, Shiva could not refuse. Bhasmasura then used this powerful boon to spread terror. His pride then turned into arrogance and he decided to kill Shiva in the hope of taking his place. Shiva had never thought of such a consequence, and turned to Vishnu for help. Vishnu turned into a beautiful maiden, Mohini, and appeared before the demon. Bhasmasura fell for her beauty and wanted to marry her. She agreed — on the condition that he convince her about his fidelity. He asked how she would be convinced. Mohini said she was easy to please. All he had to do was touch his forehead and swear that he would always be faithful to her. In his enthusiasm he did just that… and was instantly reduced to ashes.

Vaishnavites and Shaivites

All Hindu religious literature confirms that the Hindu Trinity always worked as a perfect team. Since greater importance is placed on the responsibilities of Vishnu and Shiva, there are innumerable instances when Vishnu would invoke the blessings and support of Shiva, and whenever necessary Shiva would invoke the blessings of Vishnu. Yet we find that even amongst

Hindus, there are two distinct groups. The followers of Vishnu and his many forms are known as Vaishnavites, and the followers of Shiva and his many forms are known as Shaivites. There is yet another group, known as Shakts, that believes in the power of the female energy described as Shakti.

Who is the Most Important?

The members of the Hindu Trinity fulfil specific, well-defined responsibilities. Many wonder whether the responsibility of one is more important than that of the other two. One day, sages and saints were perplexed on discussing this issue. They asked the sage Bhrigu, son of Brahma, to visit the three gods and present his observations.

Bhrigu decided to visit his father first. Brahma was happy to see his son, but since Bhrigu did not greet him appropriately, nor show any reverence, Brahma was angry and walked away without talking to Bhrigu.

Bhrigu next visited Kailash to meet Shiva, who was happy to see him and wanted to embrace him in welcome. However, Bhrigu was rude and said, "I will not embrace you. You do not follow the rules of simple courtesy and good manners." This statement infuriated Shiva. He chased Bhrigu with his trident to punish him for this audacity.

Bhrigu then went to Vaikunth to meet Vishnu. Vishnu was sleeping at the time. Bhrigu waited impatiently near Vishnu's bed, hoping he would wake up but he did not. After waiting awhile, Bhrigu lost his temper and kicked Vishnu in the chest. Vishnu awoke with a start, and finding Bhrigu standing there, he touched Bhrigu's feet and gently said, "Honoured sage, my chest is hard. Your feet are delicate. Did I hurt your foot?" The sage felt ashamed at Vishnu's kind and gentle behaviour. Vishnu respectfully offered Bhrigu a comfortable seat to sit on. Bhrigu was flattered and content.

On returning to the sages and saints, Bhrigu conveyed that Vishnu was the most outstanding of the gods.

There is one definite lesson all humankind can learn from the working of the gods. It does not matter what the source of power is — physical strength, knowledge or a special ability. Power in all its forms needs to be used with caution. Well utilized, it grows. When misused, it destroys. This truth is equally valid for gods as well as human beings.

5

Brahma

BRAHMA

Brahma is the first member of the Hindu Trinity. Born from a golden egg in water, Brahma is the seed of all creation, the uncreated creator. Being born from water, he is also known as **Kanja** (*born in water*). Many believe that a lotus emerged from Vishnu's navel and Brahma sprang from the lotus. For this reason, he is also known as **Nabhija** (*born from the navel*).

Brahma should not be confused with **Brahman**, the Supreme Being, or the Supreme Cosmic Spirit of Hinduism. Brahma fulfils the responsibility of creating the universe on behalf of Brahman. Some say that Brahma is the son of the Supreme Being, Brahman and the female energy, Maya.

Brahma is usually depicted standing or sitting on a lotus. He has four heads facing the four quarters of the world. The heads represent the knowledge of the four Vedas, the four yugas, or eras, and the four castes based upon individual vocations. The faces are bearded, and the eyes are closed in meditation. He has four arms often shown holding a rosary, *kusha* grass, a spoon or ladle, a *kamandal* (water pot) or a book. The rosary is symbolic of time. The water in the kamandal is symbolic of creation. The spoon/ladle and the kusha grass are symbols of offerings and sacrifices. The book symbolizes all kinds of knowledge. The hand that holds nothing signifies protection, or a blessing.

Brahma's vehicle is a swan, a bird that is believed to have the power to separate milk and water. This is symbolic of the power to discriminate between righteousness and evil. Sometimes, Brahma is shown riding a chariot drawn by seven swans.

As part of his responsibility, Brahma created ten Prajapatis, or fathers of the human race. They are mentioned in the **Manusmriti** as **Marichi**, **Atri**, **Angirasa**, **Pulastya**, **Pulaha**, **Kratu**, **Vasishtha**, **Prachetas** or **Daksh**, **Bhrigu** and **Narad**. He also created the **Saptrishi**, or seven sages. Since these were born from the mind of Brahma, they are known as mind-sons, or **Manas Putras**. Together, the ten Prajapatis and the Saptrishi helped Brahma create the universe.

Brahma's consort is Saraswati, and they reside in Brahmapura, located on Mount Meru. While Brahma is said to represent the Vedas, Saraswati represents their spirit and meaning. Therefore, all knowledge and spiritual thought has come through their grace. They are also the origin of music, dance, theatrical art and stagecraft.

Worship of Brahma

Of the three gods that form the Hindu Trinity, Vishnu and Shiva are universally revered. Brahma is worshipped only on special occasions.

The sages once decided to organize a great *yagya*. Bhrigu was appointed the presiding priest. The sages also decided that the greatest among gods would be invited as the presiding deity. Bhrigu was entrusted the responsibility of choosing one from amongst the Trinity. When Bhrigu went to meet Brahma, he found him so engrossed in hearing the music being played by Saraswati that he did not notice Bhrigu, who was trying to attract his attention. The infuriated Bhrigu cursed Brahma that no person would worship him. To this day, Brahma is not worshipped the way Vishnu and Shiva are revered. While there are thousands of temples dedicated to Vishnu and Shiva, there is only one major temple dedicated to Brahma — near Pushkar Lake in Rajasthan.

Every year, on *Kartik Purnima* (full-moon night in the Hindu month *Kartik*), there are special celebrations when thousands of pilgrims visit the temple and bathe in the lake. Two other temples exist, in Mangalwedha (Solapur, Maharashtra) and in Kumbakonam (Thanjavur, Tamil Nadu). The smaller temples are not of much importance. However, an idol of Brahma is placed in the temples where the principal deity is Vishnu or Shiva because together they represent Brahman, the Supreme Being.

Brahma and Vishnu

Brahma and Vishnu once approached Shiva to enquire about his beginning and end. Brahma was to find the beginning, and Vishnu the end. Both set out to accomplish their mission, but neither could succeed. Vishnu went to Shiva and acknowledged him as a part of Brahman, the Supreme Being. Brahma did not want to accept that he was unable to trace out Shiva's beginning. He compelled a flower to bear false witness that Brahma was aware of Shiva's

beginning. Shiva could not be deceived. He felt hurt by Brahma's deviousness, and cursed that no one would worship him.

Brahma and Shiva

When Brahma was creating the universe, he created a beautiful female deity with many charming forms. He called her **Satrupa**. Enamoured by her beauty, Brahma could not help staring at her, compelling the embarrassed Satrupa to move from one place to another. Brahma grew five heads to look in all the four directions, and also above him. Shiva did not like this. He felt that since Brahma had created Satrupa, she was his daughter, and it was wrong on his part to embarrass her in this way. In anger, Shiva cut off one of Brahma's heads to punish him and remind him that his intentions were immoral. He also cursed Brahma that he would never be worshipped as a god. The repentant Brahma has been reciting the four Vedas ever since.

However, theologians believe that at one time, Brahma was equally revered. Over time, Vaishnavites and the Shaivites became dominant, eclipsing worship of Brahma.

Pleasing Brahma

Of the three members of the Hindu Trinity, Brahma is the easiest to please. Prayer, sacrifices and austerities easily please him. Irrespective of whether one is a god, demon or man, Brahma is known to grant boons easily. The Hindu scriptures reveal that many of these boons were misused, forcing Vishnu and Shiva to intervene and stop the damage.

Vishnu

VISHNU

No other Hindu god has as many devotees as Vishnu. Hindu religious books portray him reclining comfortably on the serpent Sheshnag, whose thousand-headed hood provides an umbrella over him. His consort, Lakshmi, is seated beside him. He is sometimes depicted sleeping on the coils of the serpent.

The name *Vishnu* is derived from the root word *vish*, which means *to pervade*. As a god, Vishnu pervades all things and beings, residing in the latter as the soul — the life force. Once the life force withdraws, the body perishes. By extension, this makes every being a home of god.

Vishnu is depicted with a dark blue complexion, one head and four arms. In his hands he carries the Sudarshan *Chakra* (discus), a *gada* (mace) named Kaumodki, a conch-shell named Panchjanya and a lotus. His face is always calm and peaceful. He wears a golden crown on his head, and a *vana-mala* (garland) around the neck. Bedecked with precious gems and jewellery, the jewel Kaustubh adorns his chest, and the Syamantak gem gleams on his wrist. Garuda is his vehicle.

Whenever evil grew beyond tolerance, Vishnu incarnated to protect his devotees. He has 24 incarnations. Of these, 10 are especially significant, with the last yet to come. Vishnu has a thousand names. Devotees are free to remember him by whatever name and form they like. Vishnu resides in Vaikunth.

Incarnations of Vishnu

The first incarnation (*avatar*) of Vishnu was in the form of a fish — **Matsya**. At the end of the first era, the demon Hayagriv stole the Vedas from Brahma and hid them at the bottom of the sea. Taking the form of Matsya, Vishnu forewarned Manu Vaivasvat that a deluge would come and he should protect the seeds of plants and pairs of living beings. Vaivasvat followed the instructions. Everything was destroyed except what was in the ark, and the cycle of creation started again. The story of a global flood is found in many religions; archaeologists maintain that traces of such a catastrophe exist.

The second incarnation of Vishnu was in the form of a giant tortoise — **Kacchap** or **Kurm** — whose role in bearing a mountain on his back as the gods and *Asuras* churned the ocean during *Samudramanthan* in search of amrit — the nectar of immortality — is described a little later.

The third incarnation of Vishnu was in the form of a boar — **Varah**. The demon Hiranyaksa had abducted and taken Bhumi (Earth) to the depths of the ocean. Enraged at this action, Vishnu intervened in the form of a boar — Varah. Jumping into the ocean, he lifted Bhumi with his tusks and brought her to the surface of the water. Bhumi then assumed her beautiful form, and Varah killed Hiranyaksa.

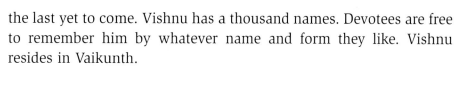

The fourth incarnation of Vishnu was in the form of a half-man, half-lion — **Narasimha**. Hiranyakasipu was furious at Vishnu for having killed his twin brother Hiranyaksa. He offered great penance, sacrifices and prayers to Brahma who granted him a boon. Hiranyakasipu sought that neither god, nor man or animal should be able to kill him. He should not die inside a house, or outside, nor should he die on the ground or in the sky. No weapon should kill him. Protected by this boon, Hiranyakasipu became bold and arrogant. He forbade prayers to Vishnu. No one was to even utter his name. However, his own son Prahlad was a great devotee of Vishnu. He refused to comply with his father's orders. Enraged at his son's behaviour, Hiranyakasipu asked him to summon Vishnu from a pillar in the court. Breaking the pillar, Vishnu emerged as Narasimha, put Hiranyakasipu on his lap and tore him apart with his claws, thus ending yet another evil period.

The fifth incarnation of Vishnu was in the form of **Vaman**, a dwarf. The demon king Bali had defeated Indra and other gods, and taken over control of the three worlds. Incarnating as Vaman, Vishnu approached Bali and begged for as much land as he could cover in just three steps. Amused that a dwarf wanted land equal to three of his small steps, Bali granted the request... and Vaman began to grow. In one step he covered the whole earth, and in the second, the heavens, leaving no place for the third step. Bali bent his head so that Vaman could place the third step on it. Vaman pushed him with his foot, sending Bali down to *Patal Lok* — the netherworld. Indra was once again the ruler of the universe.

The sixth incarnation of Vishnu was in the form of the sage **Parasuram**. As an obedient son, Parasuram once beheaded his mother to please his father. Later, when his father's anger had cooled, he offered a boon to Parasuram, who asked for his mother's life. On another occasion, the father asked him to bring back a cow and calf stolen by King Kartavirya and his party. In the fierce battle that ensued between the king and Parasuram, Kartavirya and many of his sons died. Parasuram brought back the cow and the calf. However, some of King Kartavirya's sons killed Parasuram's father. His mother told him what had happened, beat her chest 21 times and jumped

into her husband's funeral pyre. Enraged at the double tragedy, Parasuram vowed to go around the world 21 times and destroy the Kshatriya race.

The seventh incarnation of Vishnu was in the form of **Ram**. He is referred to as *Maryada Purushottam Ram*. Son of Dashrath and Kaushalya, Ram is a household word not only in India, but also in many other countries. Ram was a very capable and just king. He established *Ram Rajya* — an ideally ruled kingdom. Valmiki has recorded his life in the Ramayan, running into 24,000 verses that eulogize the classic triumph of good over evil.

Krishna is the eighth incarnation of Vishnu. Born as the eighth (and first surviving) son of Vasudev and Devki, he was brought up along with his half-brother Balram by foster parents Nand and Yashoda in Gokul. Kansa, who then ruled at Mathura, made several futile attempts to kill Krishna. Ultimately, Krishna killed Kansa. Krishna is revered for the moral guidance he provided. He linked moral conduct not only with one's actions, but also with one's objective in life.

The ninth incarnation of Vishnu was in the form of **Buddha**, also known as *The Enlightened One,* or simply Gautam Buddha. Son of King Shudhodhan, he spent a sheltered childhood, but shocked by his first sight of suffering and death, he renounced the world to seek the truth. He spread the message of love, peace, non-violence and moderation in all things. His teachings gave birth to Buddhism, a major religion that is no longer that popular in India as it is in large parts of the Far East.

Some religious thinkers consider Balram as the ninth incarnation of Vishnu, not Buddha. However, Buddha is the popular choice.

The tenth incarnation of Vishnu — **Kalki** — has yet to come. It is believed that when human degeneration reaches its nadir, Kalki will appear to protect the good souls, who alone shall survive the end of the world. After this apocalypse, a new world cycle will commence, with another Satyayug.

People with a scientific outlook consider the many incarnations of Vishnu as representing various phases in the process of evolution, as described by Darwin. However, the sages insist that Vishnu incarnated in different forms to fulfil prevailing needs.

Samudramanthan

Samudramanthan literally means *churning of the ocean*. Indra, the king of gods, once showed disrespect to the sage Durvasa and, cursed by him, lost everything to the demons. Frustrated at their defeat, the gods went to Vishnu to seek help. Vishnu advised them to ignore the defeat, befriend the demons, and churn the ocean to obtain *amrit*, the elixir of immortality.

Using the mountain Mandar as a churner and the serpent Vasuki as a rope, the gods and the demons churned the ocean. Meanwhile Kurm, an incarnation of Vishnu, prevented the mountain from sinking into the ocean,

The first thing that arose from the ocean was *halahala,* a deadly poison. If spilled, it would have destroyed the whole world. Shiva quickly swallowed it, but the poison turned his throat blue. This is why Shiva is also known as **Neelkanth**.

Thereafter, the churning yielded the celestial cow **Kamadhenu**, the wish-fulfilling tree **Kalpvriksha**, the elephant **Airavata**, and the white horse **Uchaisrava**. The sages took Kamadhenu, Indra took Airavata and planted Kalpvriksha in heaven. Bali, the king of demons, had an eye on Uchaisrava. When the precious jewel **Kaustubh** was recovered, Vishnu wore it on his chest.

Then emerged **Lakshmi**, the goddess of fortune, **Sura**, the goddess of wine and **Dhanvantri**, physician to the gods. His hands held the amrit in a vessel. Lakshmi immediately decided to live in Vishnu's chest. Surprisingly, the demons were reluctant to accept Sura. So Indra took her. However, despite an earlier agreement that the gods and the demons would share the amrit equally, the demons snatched the vessel from Dhanvantri. The gods protested, but the demons would not agree to share it.

Vishnu then took the form of a beautiful maiden, Mohini. She bewitched the demons and lured them to place the vessel in her hands. Vishnu then distributed the amrit amongst the gods only. Once they gained immortality, the gods attacked and defeated the demons and regained the heavens.

The churning of the ocean is analogous to the churning of one's mind. Just as the gods and the demons churned the ocean to get things, so do good and bad thoughts (like amrit or halahala) emerge from the mind… the former leads to immortality, while the latter destroys us. Opposing human compulsions are mirrored in Shiva's altruistic act of consuming the poison, and in the demons' blatantly selfish actions. The good may suffer temporarily, but always emerge successful in the long run.

Char Dham Yatra

Just as there are four Vedas, four castes and four eras in the Hindu tradition, there are four important places of pilgrimage. It is the pious aspiration of every devout Hindu to perform the *Char Dham Yatra* in his lifetime, since it is believed to ensure a place in heaven. *Char* means *four*, *Dham* denotes *the abode of a deity*, *Yatra* is a *pilgrimage*. Together, *Char Dham*

Yatra means *a pilgrimage to the four important abodes of Hindu gods.* It is a challenge to visit all the four Dhams. Besides the spiritual influence of a visit to each of these four powerful deities, one gains through the long travel and interaction with people who look, eat and speak differently. Significantly, of the four deities, three are dedicated to Vishnu, and only one to Shiva.

Jagannath Puri is described as a heavenly pilgrimage. *Jagannath* literally means *the master of the universe,* viz., Vishnu. The deity in the temple is that of Vishnu/Krishna. Alongside the main deity, there are idols of Balram and Subhadra.

Dwarka is an ancient city of historic and religious importance. After leaving Mathura, Sri Krishna moved to Dwarka, making it the capital of the Yadavas. Dwarkapeeth was established by Adi Shankaracharya to promote *Sanatan Dharma*. Here, Sri Krishna reigns supreme. In the **Skand Purana**, Prabhaskhand, it is mentioned that the deity at Dwarka is very benevolent. Even those who are born as bacteria, insects, birds, animals and reptiles are absolved of their sins and attain salvation.

Badrinath is situated deep within the Himalayas, between the peaks Nar and Narayan, alongside the Alaknanda River. The beauty of Badrinath has been described in the Mahabharat, Skand Purana and several other Hindu religious texts. The principal deity is Vishnu. Made of Shalgram stone, the idol is artistically carved. Adi Shankaracharya located the idol

in a nearby pond in the 7th century. When the perennial Alaknanda is freezing cold, people bathe in hot springs alongside the river.

Rameshwaram is the only Dham dedicated to Shiva. The Ramayan says it was here that Sri Ram bathed and offered prayers to Shiva before he advanced to wage war against Ravan. It was in the Kotandarmar temple that Ravan's brother Vibhishan surrendered to Sri Ram and sought his protection. In the Dhanushkoti temple, there are idols of Ram, Sita, Lakshman, Hanuman and Vibhishan.

Vishnu and Lakshmi

Vishnu's consort, Lakshmi, is often shown sitting besides Vishnu, pressing his legs to comfort him as he reclines majestically on the coils of Sheshnag. Lakshmi is inseparable from Vishnu, and follows wherever he goes. When Vishnu is shown standing on a lotus, she is shown on his left, also standing on a lotus. She believed to be Vishnu's spouse whenever he incarnates. She was Padma, or Kamla, as Vaman's consort, Dharani as Parasuram's consort, Sita as Sri Ram's consort and Rukmini as Sri Krishna's consort.

Vishnu and Sheshnag

Vishnu is always depicted reclining or seated on the coils of Sheshnag, with the thousand-headed hood of Sheshnag serving as a parasol. Vishnu and Sheshnag are dear to each other. Whenever Vishnu incarnates, Sheshnag accompanies to provide support and service. He served as younger brother Lakshman to Sri Ram. The Ramayan speaks of his glories. His supportive role as Krishna's elder brother Balram is glorified in many Hindu scriptures.

Vishnu and Garuda

Vishnu travels on his vehicle, Garuda, a powerful bird resembling an eagle. He is symbolic of the power and speed with which Vishnu reaches wherever required. He resides with Vishnu in every place of worship. It may seem strange that while Vishnu reclines on the coils of Sheshnag, a snake, his vehicle is a bird of prey. In everyday life, the two are natural enemies, but here, they represent the harmonious blend of these two forces in Vishnu, symbolizing the power he exerts over all beings, which are verily sustained by him.

Vishnu and Shalgram

In Nepal, on the banks of the river Gandki, one comes across smooth, shining, black, egg-like stones that may have a hole, or be like a shell, or have round white lines or designs on them. Known as Shalgram, these are black stones with fossil ammonite. Devotees of Vishnu consider them sacred. Religious texts mention that no Hindu home is complete without a Shalgram.

The **Padma Purana** says that a home with a Shalgram is like a place of pilgrimage. One is absolved of major sins by looking at a Shalgram. Those who pray to it are specially blessed.

In the **Skand Purana**, Shiva has narrated the importance of Shalgram. Every year on the twelfth day of the Hindu month *Kartik*, women conduct marriages between a Shalgram and Tulsi. Amongst Hindus, this connotes the start of the marriage season.

The **Brahmavaivarta Purana**, Prakritikhand, chapter 21, says that Vishnu and Lakshmi reside wherever one finds a Shalgram. Shalgram has the power to bless one with important positions, property and prosperity, as well as absolve all kinds of sins.

It is believed that sprinkling water that has been in contact with Shalgram is a great blessing. The touch of Shalgram promotes philanthropy. Offering of prayers is like reading the Vedas. Whoever offers prayers to Tulsi, Shalgram and the conch shell shall always be dear to Vishnu.

7

Shiva

SHIVA

Shiva is the third member of the Hindu Trinity. Just as Brahma is responsible for the creation and Vishnu for sustenance, Shiva is responsible for the destruction or dissolution of the universe. After the disintegration of the universe, there is a haunting void, followed by regeneration of the universe once again. Shiva, therefore, destroys and also regenerates. Contrary to what many think, Shiva is a positive force that destroys evil and regenerates virtue. The cycle continues era after era by the gods of the Hindu Trinity. Shiva is said to be *Anaadi* (without a beginning) and *Anant* (without an end).

Shiva is often called **Bhola Nath** or **Bhole Nath**. *Bhola* means *innocent, simple-hearted, unsophisticated. Bhole* is pronounced differently, but has a similar meaning. *Nath* means *master.* Together, the two words mean *a simple-hearted master.* Some also take the name to mean the Good One, or the Pure One. The repetition of the name purifies an individual.

Shiva is worshipped as the *Linga,* or *Lingam,* meaning the phallus. Since mankind prefers to see everything in its own form, Shiva is depicted as good-looking, youthful and of very fair complexion. The limbs are strong and smooth, but smeared with ash. He has three eyes, the third one being located between the eyebrows. There are three horizontal lines on his forehead. The thick coil of his long and matted hair is piled like a crown on the head. The river Ganga emerges from this topknot, and the crescent moon adorns his head as a diadem. He has four arms; one carries a *damaru* (a little drum), one a *trishul* (trident), while the other two hands offer protection and blessings respectively. He is clad in garments made of tiger, deer and elephant

skins. While coiled snakes are his necklace, girdle, bracelets — the *yagyopavit*, a garland of skulls — adorns his blue neck. He wears wristbands of *Rudraksh* beads. He is often depicted as sitting with his eyes closed in serene meditation. His face radiates the peace and tranquillity of the ascetic.

The description does not make Shiva as attractive as one would like him to be, but each of the attributes expresses his glory. The matted hair on his head reminds one of Vayu, the Wind God, representing the vital air that no living being in this world can do without. The Ganga flowing from his topknot symbolizes the control Shiva has over the Holy Ganga and its life-giving waters. The fifth day crescent moon symbolizes Shiva's control over Time as well his power to destroy and re-create. The third eye on his forehead is symbolic of the wisdom and energy that destroys evil and the sinners. The *vibhuti* on the forehead signifies the transitory nature of material things, immortality of the soul and the glory of the Lord.

While the use of tiger skin is symbolic of Shiva's control over Shakti, and his victory over lust, the use of elephant skin is symbolic of his control over pride. The use of deerskin signifies control over the mind. The ashes smeared on the body remind one that death is the ultimate reality of life. One comes from the earth and returns to it after death. The use of *Rudraksh* signifies control over health and welfare. The deadly serpents around his neck and the body signify Shiva's victory over death. The *damaru* is representative of the universal sound 'Om', the source of language and expression. Shiva's *trishul* is a reminder of the functions of the Hindu Trinity — creation, sustenance and dissolution.

Shiva's consort is Parvati, daughter of Himavant, and they are blessed with two sons, Ganesh and Kartikeya. Nandi, a bull, is his choice of a vehicle. They reside at Mount Kailash, deep in the Himalayas.

Shiva as a Dancer

Shiva is known to be a great musician, dancer and master of several arts. As all forms of dance are believed to have sprung from him, he is known as **Nataraj,** the king of dancers. It is said that he dances every evening to the great pleasure of those who visit him at Kailash. In his celestial dance, he is shown with four arms and two legs in a classic dance pose, holding the damaru in the upper right arm and fire in the upper left arm. The lower right arm is in a protective

posture while the left lower arm points at the leg. The left foot rests on the demon Apasamara-purusa.

Shiva's dance is symbolic of the process of creation, sustenance and destruction. While the damaru symbolizes sound, a principle of creation, the fire denotes destruction. The demon Apasamara-purusa under his foot is symbolic of the ignorance that creates havoc; the two lower arms reflect that whoever is devoted to Shiva has nothing to fear.

Names of Shiva

Like Vishnu, Shiva is also known by a thousand names. The **Shiva Sahasranama** lists 1008 names, while the **Shiva Purana** lists 108 of the more popular names. Each name has a meaning. For instance, the names **Mahadev** and **Maheshwar** both mean the Supreme God. **Mahabaleshwar** means God of great strength. **Rameshwar** means the God worshipped by Sri Ram. **Mahakal** means one who has conquered time. **Trinetra**, **Triaksha** and **Triayana** mean one who has three eyes. **Shankar** means one who gives joy. **Shambu** means that he is the abode of joy. **Pashupatinath** means the Lord of all creatures. Just as many of his names describe his attributes and benevolence, there are also names that describe his power to destroy. **Bhairav** means the frightful one. **Ekambaranath** means the destroyer of evil. Since he sits facing south as he teaches, he is known as **Dakshinmurti**. The thousand names describe the multifaceted personality of Shiva.

Shiva and Brahma

In the **Bhagavata Purana**, it is explained that Shiva manifested in many forms from the forehead of Brahma, who was aggrieved when his sons refused to create progeny to inhabit the universe. A son then appeared from the disappointed Brahma's forehead, and split into two portions, one a male and the other a female. When the male child started crying uncontrollably, Brahma named him Rudra. The child cried seven more times, and each time, Brahma gave him a new name. The eight names are: **Rudra**, **Sharva**, **Bhava**, **Ugra**, **Bhim**, **Pashupati**, **Ishana** and **Mahadev**. These eight names are associated with the earth, water, fire, wind, sky, Kshetragya (a yogi), the sun, and the moon respectively. The child was Shiva and was asked to create progeny. However, when Brahma observed Shiva's unique powers, he asked him to observe austerities instead. In the **Shiva Purana**, it is explained that Shiva told Brahma that he would create an identical form known as Rudra.

Shiva and Vishnu

Although Shiva and Vishnu are two distinct members of the Hindu Trinity, and each has a different responsibility, the two are known to be very devoted to each other.

When Sri Ram and Lakshman were looking for Sita, who had been abducted by Ravan, Shiva's consort Dakshayani was overtaken by doubt when Shiva called Sri Ram the Master of the Universe. To prove Shiva wrong, Dakshayani disguised herself as Sita and went before Sri Ram and Lakshman. They immediately recognised her true form, much to her embarrassment. On returning to Shiva, she persisted in hiding the truth from him. Hurt by her suspicious temperament and behaviour, Shiva decided to forego an intimate relationship with her. If she

could not respect Vishnu, he could not hold her dear. Frustrated with the situation, she invoked the support of Sri Ram, pleading that it would be best that she give up her life. Soon thereafter she visited her father's home, once again against Shiva's advice to attend a yagya where everyone was invited, but not Shiva. She thought it was only through oversight. However, on arrival she found it was intentional. She felt insulted and ended her life in the yagya. She was reborn as Parvati to Himavant and Mena, and after many austerities and penances was remarried to Shiva.

Just as Shiva is devoted to Vishnu, Vishnu is equally devoted to Shiva. Just before Sri Ram was to cross over the sea to go to Lanka to put an end to Ravan's rule, Sri Ram invoked the blessings of Shiva. He built a *Shivalinga* of sand and offered prayers. A magnificent temple stands at Rameshwaram, one of the four major places of pilgrimage for all Hindus.

One comes across many instances of the devotion both Shiva and Vishnu have for each other. When Vishnu incarnated as Parasuram, Shiva gave him his axe. It was Shiva's bow that Sri Ram strung and broke at Sita's *swayamvar*. Shiva proclaims the glory of Vishnu, and Vishnu in turn reveres Shiva. It is said that Shiva utters the name of Vishnu in the ears of his devotees at the time of death. This ensures them a place in Vaikunth.

Shiva and Parvati

Soon after Parvati was born to Himavant and Mena, Narad came to congratulate the proud parents. The parents placed the baby girl at Narad's feet and enquired what was in store for her. He talked of the great glory that awaited her, but said she would be married to an ascetic, one who walked about almost naked, detached from the world. He also added that the only person he knew with that description was Shiva. He could only be won over through penance and austerities. The parents felt shocked at the prediction.

When Mena went to Parvati, her daughter told her softly, "Mother, I had a vision wherein a Brahmin has advised that I should practise austerity. Austerity brings great joy and happiness. It was through penance that the universe was created. It is through penance that Vishnu preserves this universe. It is through austerity and penance that one attains what one desires."

Parvati left home to offer penance in the name of Lord Shiva. She was too delicate to observe such severe austerities and penance, but her mind was steadfast on the feet of Lord Shiva. Rigorous fasting emaciated her body. It is not known for how long this continued. One day, she heard the voice of Brahma telling her that she should end her austerities, as her wish would soon be granted. She should return home when her father came to fetch her. She should also respond positively when the seven sages met her.

Meanwhile, Shiva moved from one place to another telling the sages of the virtues of Sri Ram. One day, Sri Ram appeared before him and told him that none but he could have lived by the exemplary vow he had taken. He told him of the birth of Parvati, and how she had practised austerities and penance in complete devotion to him. Sri Ram then desired that Shiva grant him the boon that he would marry Parvati. Shiva explained that he could not refuse one whom he held in such high reverence.

When the seven sages called upon Shiva, he said, "Go to Parvati and put her love to test. Then ask her father to call her back home and dispel her doubts."

When the seven sages called upon Parvati they wanted to know the purpose of the austerities and penance she had gone through. She politely responded, "I am shy to admit to you. I have always desired to have Lord Shiva as my husband."

The sages laughed. "You seek a husband who roams about naked and shameless, one who has no family. He had once married Daksahyani, but left her to die. He lives on alms. Can a woman ever live with such a person?" the sages asked. Parvati was not convinced. "We have an excellent match for you," the sages continued. "He is good looking and friendly. Everyone sings of his glory. He is the lord of Lakshmi and lives in Vaikunth."

"I would rather die than give up my vow," Parvati was adamant. "My Lord Shiva may have no virtues as compared to Vishnu, but I know only him who makes me happy. Either I marry him, or remain single."

On seeing Parvati's firm devotion, the sages rejoiced: "Glory to you, Mother of the Universe! Shiva is the lord, and you the Mother of the Universe!" They bowed before her and left to meet her father to take her back home.

Shiva and Parvati were married to enjoy eternal bliss. Hindu men and pray for connubial bliss matching that of Shiva and Parvati. Unmarried young men and women fast on Mondays, praying to them that they may be blessed with good spouses and enjoy married life just like them.

Shiva and Parvati are inseparable. Parvati is Shakti — the divine universal power. There can be no Shiva without Shakti. And there can be no Shakti without Shiva. Together, they are symbolic of the divine union of power and devotion.

Shiva and his Sons

Shiva and Parvati had two sons — Ganesh and Kartikeya. We have already discussed about the elephant-headed god Ganesh. Kartikeya was conceived with the purpose of putting an end to the terror created by the demon Tarakasura.

The combined power of the gods could not control him. He was invincible. In desperation, the gods sought the advice of Brahma, who said only a son of Shiva and Parvati could kill him. At that time they were not married. Shiva was roaming in the forests and Parvati was offering penance and austerities. The gods sent Kama, the god of love, to arouse desire in Shiva's mind for Parvati. When Shiva opened his third eye, Kama was reduced to ashes.

Later, when Shiva and Parvati were married, the gods approached Shiva to tell him how Tarakasura was creating terror for everyone. They also told him that only their son could vanquish him.

Shiva then created a form with five faces, a spark emerging from the third eye of each face. Agni and Vayu carried these sparks and released them into the river Ganga, wherefrom they went to a pond where five forest maidens, krittikas (pleiades) found them. The sparks transformed into children. Each of the five maidens suckled them. When Shiva and Parvati reached there with Agni, Vayu, Ganga and other gods there was confusion as to who had a right over the children. Parvati desired to have them but was unsure as to how she could feed five children simultaneously. To end the confusion, the five children merged into a single child. Shiva gave him five names to satisfy the five parents. This child had six heads instead of five, the sixth one acting to unite the five attributes of the father's power into one being. The five attributes refer to the five senses, and the sixth is the mind that controls them. He was named **Kartikeya**. The gods blessed him with special powers and weapons, and made him the chief commander of their forces. Later, he killed Tarakasura.

Kartikeya is also known as **Kumar**, **Skand**, **Mahasen** and **Guh**. Kartikeya was married to Devsena, the daughter of the sage Kashyap. Garuda gave Kartikeya the gift of his son, a peacock, to serve as his vehicle. Kartikeya moved to the southern part of India, where he is well known as **Subramanya** and **Murugan**. Several temples, many of them on hilltops, are dedicated to him.

Shiva and Ganga

Shiva is always portrayed with the river Ganga flowing out of his hair. Ganga lived in the heavens and was brought down to earth through great penance by King Bhagirath who desired that the sixty thousand sons of King Sagar killed by the wrath of the sage Kapil might attain salvation. To prevent destruction from the uncontrolled waters of the Ganga falling upon earth, Shiva agreed to accept her on his head to break the force of the fall. Ganga thought the force would push Shiva into the ground. To humble Ganga, Shiva engulfed her in his hair. It was only after further pleadings by Bhagirath that Shiva allowed Ganga to flow out of his topknot. Ganga is said to be Parvati's sister. Since the sparks emitted by Shiva were carried by Ganga to the five damsels, Ganga is also referred to as Kartikeya's mother.

Shiva and his Devotees

Shaivites are totally devoted to Shiva. They believe that he is the Supreme Being. They assert that Brahma and Vishnu serve under his guidance.

There are many other devotees who accept him as part of the Hindu Trinity. He is easy to please through prayer, sacrifice and penance. For this reason, he is also known as **Ashutosh**, meaning *one who can be pleased easily.* The sage Markandey is known to be one of his most ardent devotees.

In **Padma Purana** it is explained that the sage Markandey composed the *Mahamrituanjaya Mantra* in hymn form. The sage Mrikandu did not have any children. To please Shiva, both he and his wife endured great penance and sacrifice. Pleased with them, Shiva appeared before them and said, "You will be blessed with a son. If you want a capable, knowledgeable, renowned and religious son he will live only for 16 years. If you want a son devoid of capability, he would live a 100 years. The choice is yours."

The sage Mrikandu bowed before Shiva and said, "I want a capable son even though his life may be short. What good is a son who is not capable?"

"So be it," Shiva blessed the couple and left.

Mrikandu named his son Markandey. Right from birth, he was devoted to Shiva. He composed many slokas and hymns in his childhood. Amongst the important ones was the *Mahamrituanjaya Mantra*. When Markandey completed 15 years, Mrikandu remembered what Shiva had said. He was worried. When Markandey asked the cause of the worry, Mrikandu explained it to him. Markandey said that he would pray to Shiva and seek his blessings to become immortal.

As Markandey completed the 16th year, Yama stood before him. Markandey explained that he desired to complete the chanting of the *Mahamrituanjaya Mantra*, and requested him to wait a little. But Yama was impatient. Stubborn as always, Yama prepared to snatch Markandey's life, who chanted uninterruptedly. An enraged Shiva then emerged from the Shivalinga. Observing the anger in Shiva's cyes, Yama released Markandey. To appease Shiva further, Yama blessed Markandey with immortality. Even though Shiva had personally confirmed that Markandey would die at the age of 16, Markandey's unswerving devotion won him immortality.

Shrines Devoted to Shiva

There are literally thousands of shrines devoted to Shiva. In India, every town has them. Many villages also have them. However, every devotee aspires to visit **Kailash Mansarovar** deep in the Himalayas, risking a difficult journey. **Rameshwaram** is one of the four Dhams every Hindu aspires to visit. An equally difficult journey is undertaken by many devotees to visit the cave shrine at **Amarnath** in Kashmir, where the snow Lingam grows and wanes with the moon. One of the most auspicious days to visit the shrine is the full moon night falling between July and August. **Kedarnath** in the Garhwal Himalayas is yet another shrine visited by thousands of devotees each year.

Millions of devotees offer *Ganga Jal* (water from the Ganga) to their favourite shrine on *Amavasya* (dark night) falling in the second half of July. Devotees collect Ganga Jal usually from Hardwar during the previous fortnight, and then walk to their destination, enduring great hardship. The Hindu month of *Shravan* is usually marked for prayers offered to Shiva.

8

Saraswati

Saraswati

Saraswati, wife of Brahma, is the goddess of speech, learning and knowledge. As the creator's wife, she is the mother of all creations. Those who pursue music, learning and knowledge hold her in great reverence, seeking her blessings and guidance.

Saraswati literally means *one that flows.* The reference is to the river that has now vanished. It finds mention in the **Rig-Veda**, which refers to the Saraswati as a mighty river with creative, purifying and nourishing qualities. Over thousands of years, rivers change course, merge with other rivers or even run dry. Satellite images have helped trace the images of the invisible river; it still flows underground, keeping its appointment with the Ganga and Yamuna at the holy confluence of the three rivers at Prayag.

As a river, Saraswati was symbolic of the fertility of the land, and purification. In the **Devi Purana**, Saraswati has been referred to by names like **Savitri**, **Gayatri**, **Sati**, **Lakshmi** and **Ambika**. In several other ancient texts, she has been referred to by names like **Vagdevi** or **Vagisvari**, **Brahmi**, **Vani**, **Sharda**, **Bharti**, **Veenapani**, **Vidyadhari**, **Sarvmangla** and many more. She is the goddess who dispels all kinds of doubts and imparts the correct perception.

Saraswati receives great reverence from all artistes and musicians. Being the very manifestation of rhythm, tone and melody, she is remembered through the seven notes — *sa, re, ga, ma, pa, dha, ni.* She is known as Saraswati for her gift of the seven musical notes. Also known as **Svaratmika** — the soul of music — she plays the *Veena*, the Indian lute, whose playing instils stability in the mind and body and sends waves of soothing rhythms throughout the body. The tranquillity of music is focussed in the Veena.

Forms of Saraswati

Fair and charming, Saraswati is dressed in white, symbolic of purity and light. She does not wear much gold or jewellery because she prefers simplicity and austerity. She has four arms. She holds a book in one of the right hands and a rosary or lotus in one of the left hands. She holds a Veena in the other two hands and is shown sitting on a white lotus, a symbol of purity, modesty and morality. It motivates one to lead a life of detachment. The rosary is symbolic of prayer and austerity. An embodiment of virtuous intellect, book in hand, she motivates

one to acquire knowledge and wisdom. Since learning and intellect are incomplete without the fine arts, she plays the Veena to motivate one to seek inner peace and bliss from which these things originate.

When she contributes her attributes and abilities to Parvati or Durga, and appears as **Mahasaraswati**, she is shown holding a *pasa* (noose), *trishul* (trident), *chakra* (discus) or a conch shell in her hands to express her power to overcome evil.

Like Brahma, she too has a swan for a vehicle and is also known as **Hamsa-vahini**, meaning *one whose vehicle is a swan*. Sometimes, a peacock is also shown as her vehicle. A peacock is attractive. Like other attractive things that pull a person away from spiritual knowledge, the beauty of the peacock may be symbolic of *Avidya*, or knowledge of mundane things rather than that of spiritual excellence. On the other hand, it could also mean that one must first gain knowledge at lower levels before seeking it at the spiritual plane.

Incidentally, the **Rig-Veda** (6.61.7) mentions that Saraswati killed the demon Vritra, who had caused great havoc.

The **Devi Bhagwat** says that Brahma, Vishnu and Shiva revere Saraswati. The **Saraswati Stuti** reveals that Saraswati is the only goddess worshipped by gods, demons, Gandharvas (divine musicians) and Nagas alike because everyone seeks knowledge. Whoever prays to Saraswati is blessed with knowledge and intellect.

There are detailed accounts of offerings and prayers to Saraswati in **Yagyavalkya Vani Stotra** and **Vasishtha Stotra** enunciated by the sages Yagyavalkya and Vasishtha.

Saraswati's Benevolence

Brahma once asked Saraswati to reside as poetic ability within a capable person. Saraswati left home in search of an appropriate individual. When she heard Valmiki uttering a verse on seeing an injured bird, she halted. Impressed by Valmiki's extraordinary ability, she decided to take up residence within him, and through her blessings, he composed the **Ramayan**. Acclaimed all over the world, he came to be known as *Adi-kavi* — one who is eternally a poet.

In the **Ramayan** there is a mention that when Ravan's brother Kumbhkaran offered great penance to Brahma, and the time came to grant him a boon, Brahma was concerned. Even if this voracious demon did no harm other than only sitting down to eat, he could still devastate the world. Brahma therefore asked Saraswati to confuse him when he was asking the boon. Kumbhkaran had intended to ask Brahma that he should stay awake for six months in a year, and sleep only for one day. With Saraswati confusing, he asked for the opposite — the ability to sleep for six months and wake up for a day. This for Kumbhkaran's doom.

The **Markandey Purana** mentions that when the sage Jaimini was passing through the forests of Vindhya, he heard birds reciting the Vedas. Their recitation was perfect. He immediately understood that the birds were under a curse, but with Saraswati's blessings were reciting the Vedas.

Saraswati's Influence

Saraswati has often helped the gods to overcome difficult situations. The gods had asked Vishnu to end the atrocities of Ravan. To enable this, he had taken birth as Sri Ram, the eldest of the sons of King Dashrath. When the king decided to retire and hand over the kingdom to Sri Ram, the gods felt that once he became king he would get so busy with affairs of the state that he would forget the purpose of his incarnation. In sheer desperation, they sought Saraswati's help. Through a dream, she influenced Manthra, the hunch-backed maid of Dashrath's second queen, Kaikeyi. In less than twenty-four hours, the situation reversed. Sri Ram went into exile for fourteen years, and Bharat was made the king.

When Bharat returned to Ayodhya and discovered how his mother Kaikeyi and maid Manthra had manipulated the situation, he was furious. He insisted on visiting Sri Ram in the forest to apologize and request him to return to Ayodhya and become king. The preceptors, the three mothers, brother

Shatrughna and others accompanied him into the forest. Once they reached there, the atmosphere was congenial but due to his guilt, Bharat found it difficult to speak to Sri Ram. With the help of his preceptor Vasishtha, he mustered courage to speak up sincerely and convincingly.

Once again, the gods were afraid that Sri Ram would return and forget his purpose. In desperation, Indra cast a spell on the people to influence them. However, the spell had no effect upon Bharat, who was an enlightened soul. The gods then turned to Saraswati to influence Bharat, who perceived the situation correctly. She refused and left, seeing no point in interfering. Sri Ram knew what was best for everyone and convinced Bharat about the need of the situation.

Vidyarambh Sanskar

It is customary amongst Hindus to conduct the *Vidyarambh Sanskar* when a child is ready to go to school. The word *vidya* means *knowledge* and *arambh* denotes *beginning*. *Vidyarambh* therefore means *the beginning of the quest for knowledge*, i.e., the first day at school. This ceremony was initially conducted when a child was old enough to learn the mysteries of life through study of the Vedas and Upanishads. Though the learning curriculum has changed in modern times, the need for knowledge remains the same.

This ceremony invokes the blessings of Sri Ganesh, who ensures there are no obstacles, and that of Saraswati, who blesses one with knowledge. With their blessings, the child steps into the world of learning and knowledge. It is customary for the child to learn to respect the teacher, who guides the child into becoming a responsible citizen in the years to come.

Before a serious study of the Vedas, the religious texts mention an additional *Medhajanan Sanskar*. The word *Medhajanan* literally means *arousing of the intellect*. It is believed that with this ceremony the child's intellect, brilliance, knowledge and devotion are greatly enhanced. It not only helps in the study of the Vedas, but also ensures there are no obstacles.

The religious texts explain that one who is not knowledgeable is deprived of wonderful fruits like morality, wealth, love and salvation. Therefore, knowledge is indispensable.

In the **Subhashit Bhandagar**, 31/14, it is said:
Knowledge is protective like a mother. Like a father, it involves one in useful pursuits. Like a wife, it helps one to overcome problems and attain contentment. It helps make one prosperous. It helps bring recognition from all directions. Like the Kalptala (a mythological creeper that grants all wishes), it gives you everything.

Worshipping Saraswati

Saraswati is worshipped not only in temples and homes, but also in places of learning. It is customary to have an idol or photograph of Saraswati in the institution, and to offer prayers to her. In many schools, children sing hymns dedicated to Saraswati every morning before going to classes. Saraswati occupies a special position in schools where music and the fine arts are taught. It is also customary to offer prayers to Saraswati before singing and music performances.

Every year in the Hindu month *Magh* when Basant Panchmi is celebrated, it is customary to offer Saraswati special prayers. Writers, poets, doctors, lawyers and musicians make special offerings. It is believed that by doing so, inspiration and creative energy are generated from within. Besides this, one is freed from sickness, grief, worry and emotional tension. In this way, Saraswati influences one's vision and outlook on life.

From the nine days of the *Navratri* festival, three days each are devoted to Durga, Lakshmi and Saraswati. Books and musical instruments are placed near the gods. Special prayers are offered. It is believed that the goddess personally visits the shrine and blesses everything. The prayers conclude on the tenth day.

Besides Hindus, people of different faiths also revere Saraswati in one form or another.

Lakshmi

LAKSHMI

Lakshmi, the wife of Vishnu, is revered as the goddess of beauty, good fortune and prosperity. Since everyone seeks good luck and fortune, she is perhaps the most worshipped of all goddesses.

In **Goraksh Sanhita**, Guru Gorakhnath has described devotion to Lakshmi as fruitful. Sri Krishna has explained that through devotion to Lakshmi, great prosperity could be attained, just as he achieved in Dwarka.

In the **Ravan Sanhita**, Ravan has explained that devotion to Lakshmi is commendable. He learnt it from Kuber, the God of Wealth. With her blessings, he made Lanka prosperous.

At one time, Lakshmi departed from the three worlds, leaving everyone devastated. The Lord of the gods, Indra was most concerned. When Lakshmi appeared during *Samudramanthan*, Indra offered prayers that pleased her. She granted him two boons. The first was that she would never leave the three worlds. The second, she agreed that she would not forsake anyone who chanted the twelve-letter mantra given by him and repeated it devotedly during daily prayers. Thus began the practice of praying to Lakshmi.

With the welfare of humankind in view, Sri Krishna's wife Rukmini once asked Lakshmi, "Devi, what kind of people and places please you to reside within?"

Lakshmi responded, "I reside with people who speak moderately, do not lose their temper, have control over self and are efficient, devoted, grateful and generous. I like people who respect the elderly, are pure at heart and are wise, forgiving, virtuous and religious. I live with women who serve their husbands, are forgiving, truthful, balanced, simple and virtuous. They must respect the gods and Brahmins. I never leave homes where yagyas are performed, prayers and sacrifices are offered to gods, and guests are cared for."

In the **Hitopadesh**, it is said:
Whoever is enthusiastic, active, capable in his work, not addicted to vice, grateful and devotedly friendly shall find that Lakshmi voluntarily comes to reside in his home.

In the **Mahabharat,** Udyogparv, it is said:
Patience, self-control, control over the senses, compassion, gentle speech and holding no grudges against friends and others promotes glory and prosperity.

The **Sharda Tilak** states that those who desire prosperity must be truthful, must eat facing the west, and must speak gently and laughingly.

The religious texts explain that Lakshmi never resides where people wear dirty clothes, do not clean their teeth or do not take a bath, eat excessively or use abusive language, or sleep even after the sun has risen high. Lakshmi also forsakes those who wear borrowed clothes, drive another's vehicle, or have undesirable relations with other women. Lakshmi never resides with people who are lazy, short-tempered, miserly, given to addiction, are immoral, egoistic, shortsighted and use crude, abusive language.

The **Mahabharat**, Shantiparv, explains that once when King Bali opposed the Brahmins after eating offensive food, Lakshmi immediately left his palace. She emphatically said, "I detest those who are addicted, impure and restless. I am leaving Bali's palace even though he is devoted to me."

Lakshmi's Birth

Lakshmi emerged from the ocean when the gods and the demons churned it during *Samudramanthan*. Since she came from the sea, she is known as the daughter of the sea. Since the moon also emerged from the sea, he is accepted as her brother. She immediately chose Vishnu as her consort, saying she would always reside in his chest. Only Vishnu was capable of controlling *Maya* (illusion) and accepted her.

Lakshmi is described as an attractive lady with a golden complexion, who is well dressed and bedecked with precious gems and jewels. She wears a lotus garland around her neck. Motherly yet youthful, her expression is calm and peaceful. She is often shown sitting or standing on a lotus, which she adores. With her four arms, she may be holding a lotus, the bilva fruit, conch shell or the *kalash* (vessel) containing amrit. She reflects a royal temperament as well as a spiritual outlook. Very often, two elephants are shown on either side pouring water from vessels belonging to heavenly maidens.

Sometimes she is shown with eight hands holding weapons like a bow and arrow, mace, discus, or the like. This is her form as **Mahalaxmi**, an avtar of Durga.

The various things she holds are symbolic of different virtues. The lotus is symbolic of detachment and purity. The *amrit kalash* symbolizes her ability to confer immortality. The *bilva* fruit signifies the fruit of actions. Her good clothes and jewels signify prosperity. She loves everyone like a mother. Her four hands offer the devotee an opportunity to attain the four goals of life — *dharma* (righteousness), *arth* (material wealth), *kama* (pleasures of life) and *moksha* (salvation).

Lakshmi has a special affinity for the lotus. Because of her love for the lotus, many of her names are linked with it, like **Padmasundari** or **Padmamukhim** (one who is as beautiful as the lotus), **Padmakshi** (one whose eyes are as beautiful as the lotus), **Padmapriya** (one who likes the lotus), and **Padmahastam** (one who holds a lotus).

Lakshmi and Vishnu

Lakshmi's divine origin and her choice of Vishnu as her consort, are described above. With Vishnu responsible for the sustenance of the universe, Lakshmi is accepted as the mother of the universe. Since Vishnu is also known as **Narayan**, she is called **Narayani**. They are inseparable: wherever Vishnu goes, she follows, through eternity. She was **Padma** or **Kamla** as Vaman's consort, **Dharani** as Parasuram's consort, **Sita** as Sri Ram's consort and **Rukmini** as Sri Krishna's consort. As Venkateshwara's consort, she is **Alamelu**. Lakshmi is Vishnu's Shakti. While Vishnu represents masculinity, Lakshmi represents everything feminine.

When the sage Bhrigu kicked Vishnu in the chest for not paying attention to him, Lakshmi complained that he had hurt her, since she resided in Vishnu's

chest. Vishnu treated the sage with respect despite his insolent way of drawing attention to himself. In disgust, Lakshmi left Vishnu in Vaikunth and descended to the earth.

A king found Lakshmi when he was ploughing land as part of a ritual. He named her **Padmawati**. Many years later, Padmawati and her friends met a young man hunting in the forest. The friends told him that hunting was not allowed in the forest. He said he was Kannan (Krishna in Tamil), and had fallen in love with Padmawati. The friends threatened to tell the king about it. However, after some intervention, Kannan and Padmawati were married.

When Lakshmi left Vishnu, prosperity abandoned him. He told Padmawati about it. He had borrowed money from Kuber for the marriage. She said she did not mind if he would bring back Lakshmi. She returned and applied sandalwood paste on Vishnu's chest. Lakshmi and Vishnu were together again. She wanted to pay his debts, but Vishnu refused. Instead he desired that she should give so much to his devotees that they would part with some of it to him. In this way, the devotees would be happy, and he too would get what he needed. Lakshmi agreed… and to this day, **Lord Balaji** continues to be deluged with wealth showered on him at the Tirupati temple. Lakshmi is benevolent to the devotees, and in turn they share their wealth with the Lord.

Vishnu is also known as **Sriniwas**, meaning *one in whom Sri (Lakshmi) resides*. They are so intimate that even their names have been united as **Lakshminarayan**, **Sitaram**, **Radheshyam** or **Radhekrishan**.

Lakshmi and Her Devotees

Since everyone desires prosperity, all Hindus are devoted to her and seek her blessings. Every Hindu home has a picture or idol of Lakshmi. Although the majority of devotees seek her for prosperity and wealth, Lakshmi is equally the goddess of purity and divinity. Since she provides divine knowledge (*Brahma-Vidya*), she is also known as **Vidya**, meaning *knowledge*. People from all walks of life seek her blessings.

Prayers to Lakshmi

One rarely comes across a temple exclusively dedicated to Lakshmi. Wherever she appears in a temple, she is with Vishnu, sitting or standing on his left side. There are more temples dedicated to the incarnates of Vishnu than to Vishnu himself. He usually appears as a part of the Hindu Trinity, or with Lakshmi.

She is often seen with other gods. Ganesh is a popular favourite. During Diwali, every Hindu offers special prayers to Lakshmi seeking wealth and prosperity. It is believed that Lakshmi visits all homes during Diwali. As a symbolic gesture, many people paint the footprints of Lakshmi entering their homes. Though prayers are offered to Lakshmi on several occasions around the year, prayers during Diwali are the most popular. Businessmen open new account books on that day to attract her favour. Since it is customary to first offer prayers to Sri Ganesh, it is commonplace to first establish a temporary temple within the house with idols of Sri Ganesh and Lakshmi, and then offer prayers.

Since Kuber is the god of wealth, some people pray to Lakshmi and Kuber during Diwali. Sometimes, it is also said that Lakshmi was married to Kuber before she emerged from the ocean. However, most religious texts disagree with this.

There are many accounts of Lakshmi and Indra. It was Lakshmi's lotus garland that the sage Durvasa had given

Indra. Not realizing its importance, Indra gave the garland to his elephant Airavata, who trampled it. This infuriated Durvasa. He cursed that because of the insult, Lakshmi would disappear and the gods would suffer. Indra apologized, but it was not until Lakshmi emerged again that prosperity returned to the gods. Indra is the god of rain. Since rain is linked with fertility of the soil and prosperity, the link between Lakshmi and Indra can be appreciated. It is also said that since Lakshmi emerged from the sea, she has a great affinity for water. She is often depicted sitting on the banks of a river. As the god of clouds and rain, Indra, too has an affinity for water.

Lakshmi is said to be flighty and transient. She does not stay at one place for long. Since everyone desires that she stay permanently in the form of prosperity, devotees offer prayers to Lakshmi every day. Mantras that please her are chanted. It is believed that attracting Lakshmi is a secret and difficult art. This is because the sage Vishvamitra had directed that the procedures must be kept secret and taught only to a capable successor at the end of one's life.

Lakshmi and Bali

Lakshmi is also linked with demon king, Bali. The **Vishnu Purana**, **Padma Purana** and **Bhagavata Purana** narrate that during his incarnation as Vaman, after Bali had fulfilled Vaman's request, Vishnu also granted Bali a boon. To redeem the boon, Bali asked Vishnu to reside in his palace in Patal Lok. When Lakshmi heard that her husband was bonded to Bali through the boon, she was disappointed. However, she tied the sacred *rakhi* on Bali's wrist and made him a brother. When Bali asked what she desired as the customary return gift, she requested that Vishnu be freed from the boon he had granted. It is said that since then the Trinity of Brahma, Vishnu and Shiva have been taking turns to reside in Bali's palace for four months.

Lakshmi's Vehicle

When Lakshmi is with Vishnu she travels with him on Garuda — Vishnu's vehicle. When alone, she has an owl as her mount. An owl is known to sleep during the day and move only at night. For this reason it is often said that when alone, Lakshmi comes in darkness and also leaves in darkness. Only when Vishnu is with her does she come in broad daylight. This is symbolic that prosperity with righteousness and spirituality stays; by itself, prosperity is transient and ephemeral.

10

Parvati

PARVATI

Parvati, wife of Shiva, is a goddess who blesses everyone with a happy married life. As already mentioned, the union of Shiva and Parvati is the ideal that Hindu couples — particularly women — aspire to have.

Since Parvati was an incarnation of Gauri, daughter of Daksh, her name is derived from the Sanskrit word *Parvata*, meaning *mountain*. *Parvati* can therefore be taken to mean *the lady of the mountains*. Some believe that the name 'Parvati' is representative of three aspects — knowledge, will and action. These attributes make her the Mother of the Universe.

Gauri and Shiva

Brahma desired that Gauri marry Shiva. It was therefore natural for her to admire Shiva. Over the years, her devotion to Shiva grew. How she rejected all other suitors and, abandoning the luxuries of her father's palace, retired to the forest to win Shiva through devotion and austerities has already been recounted. Pleased with her devotion, Shiva agreed to marry her.

Gauri then returned home waiting for Shiva to take her as his bride. However, her father Daksh was not happy. He did not like Shiva, the ash-covered ascetic, and reluctantly gave his assent to the wedding. Gauri and Shiva made their home on Mount Kailash. Daksh was an arrogant king and, because of his dislike for Shiva, he ignored his daughter also.

When Daksh organized a grand yagya he invited all the gods, the sages and the important citizens, but ignored Shiva and Gauri. When Gauri heard about the yagya, she suggested that both of them must go. Shiva refused because there was no invitation. "Do family members need an invitation?" she argued. Shiva was unmoved. Finally, Gauri decided to go alone. "A daughter can always visit her father's home," she thought.

But when Gauri reached there, she found her father and sisters were aloof. Her mother confessed that Daksh was unhappy with her for having married Shiva. In fact, he disliked Shiva. Disgusted by her father's attitude, Gauri stood at the altar of the yagya, and not only called Daksh arrogant for his behaviour, but also questioned the other gods, including Brahma and Vishnu, about participating in the yagya without Shiva, the Master of the Universe. Then declaring that she would be born to a father who was worthy of her, she invoked her powers and jumped into the yagya fire.

Enraged at what had happened, Shiva immediately sent Virbhadra and Bhadrakali, who wrecked havoc and destroyed the yagya. They cut off Daksh's head. All those who attended were attacked. Many were slain. However, Shiva was later forgiving and all the slain came to life again. Daksh was given the head of a goat, and allowed to rule his kingdom. Thereafter, Daksh became a devotee of Shiva.

Rebirth as Parvati

Gauri's rebirth as Parvati, daughter of the king of the mountains, Himavant and his wife Mena, her penance to marry Shiva, the destruction of the demon Tarakasura by a son born to her for the purpose, and her ideal marriage to Shiva have all been related earlier.

Forms of Parvati

Just as Shiva changes form to be both benevolent and destructive, Parvati, too, changes form. She is also called **Durga**, since she killed the demon Durg. As a representation of the divine universal power, she is called **Shakti**. In her destructive form, she is the fearsome yet benevolent **Kali**. People worship her in many forms, in all of which she is the combined strength of some or all the gods. We will discuss these forms later.

Parvati is the mild form of the goddess. She is usually seen sitting on Shiva's left, in which depiction she has two hands, the right one holding a blue lotus, and her left hand hanging casually by the side. When alone, she is shown with four hands. With two hands she holds a blue and red lotus, while the other two hands offer protection and blessings. She is sometimes seen holding a conch shell or a chakra, both of which are symbols of Vishnu and could mean that he is part of the power of Shiva. Some religious texts also describe Parvati as Vishnu's sister. In the **Haryardha-murti** of Shiva, the left half is Vishnu. In the **Ardhanarishvara** form, Parvati is on the left side.

Names of Parvati

Like Vishnu and Shiva, Parvati too has a thousand names. These are recorded in the **Lalita Sahasranama**. In her first birth she was known as **Gauri** or **Dakshayani**. She is also known as **Sati, Uma, Aparna, Lalita, Shivakamini, Amba** and **Ambika**. In other forms she is **Vaishnavi, Brahmi, Aindri** and **Durga**. **Devi** is a common form of addressing the many forms she takes. She is also called **Shakti**, which literally means *strength*. In this form, she is the source of Shiva's strength.

Parvati's Sons

Shiva and Parvati were blessed with two sons — Ganesh and Kartikeya. In their own right both have special abilities. These make them worthy of worship. While every Hindu worships Sri Ganesh before starting anything, Kartikeya, who moved down south from Kailash, has many temples dedicated to his worship. Sri Ganesh is credited with swallowing the demon Anlasura, who had created terror. Kartikeya is credited with killing Tarakasura. Kartikeya is the commander of the forces of the gods against the demons.

Worshipping Parvati

Young women aspire to have a married life like Parvati's and offer her prayers that they may find a suitable husband who will shower them with love and care. In the **Ramayan**, Sita is known to have prayed at the Gauri temple just before the swayamvar. It was her secret desire that Sri Ram should string Shiva's bow and thereby win her hand in marriage.

Parvati always appears sitting or standing on Shiva's left side. Since Shiva is mostly worshipped in the form of the Linga, Parvati is positioned on one side. The temples that are dedicated to her exclusively are not in her form as Parvati, but in several other forms. Her forms as Durga and Kali are widely used in exclusive temples visited by millions of devotees each year.

Every year during *Navratri* (nine nights) that last ten days, twice a year, her devotees fast and offer prayers to her as Durga. Huge temporary places of prayer are erected, idols of the goddess installed, and prayers offered. At the end of the period young girls are offered food in the belief that this reaches the goddess. This is accompanied by singing and dancing in many parts of the country. The idols are ceremoniously carried to a river or the sea and immersed amidst chanting of prayers, seeking her blessings.

Just as Vaishnavites believe that Vishnu is the Supreme Being, and Shaivites insist that the position belongs to Shiva, those who follow Shaktism consider the Goddess the Supreme Being. Other forms are considered as her manifestations, but for many, this is a moot point.

11

Durga, Shakti and Kali

DURGA, SHAKTI AND KALI

Hinduism is incomplete without the many goddesses worshipped in numerous forms by Hindus all over the world. **Lalita Sahasranama** lists a thousand names of the goddesses, each with a special attribute. The many goddesses have their own history, appearance, character and role. Each is worshipped in her own right.

Saraswati, Lakshmi and Parvati fulfil specific responsibilities as the consorts of the Hindu Trinity. A stage arrives when more needs to be done beyond what the three consorts do. This is fulfilled when Parvati, like her consort Shiva, takes an aggressive form, and with the support of other gods and goddesses protects righteousness.

Durga, identified with Parvati, is a goddess with a beautiful form, has many hands carrying weapons, and rides a lion. She is a combination of feminine and creative energy, often called Shakti. Therefore, Durga and **Shakti** are practically synonymous, though sometimes interpreted differently.

Shakti is also described as the divine universal power or energy of a deity. This power is personified in the wife. In this way, while Saraswati is Brahma's Shakti, Lakshmi is Vishnu's Shakti and Parvati is Shiva's Shakti. Parvati's form, as representative of Shakti, is called Durga.

Durga and Mahishasura

The **Devi Mahatmyam** of the **Markandey Purana** explains that the form of Durga as a warrior was created to combat the demon Mahishasura.

Rambha, king of demons, once fell in love with a water buffalo. Mahishasura was born of this union. *Mahisha* means *buffalo*. He was blessed with the ability to change between human and buffalo forms at will. He was very powerful. Through prayers and penance, he pleased Brahma and obtained the boon that neither man nor god could kill him. With his newfound power, he began plundering the three worlds. The gods could not face the terror he unleashed. Fed up of his atrocities, the gods led by Indra went to Brahma. He took them to Vishnu and Shiva for help. Unfortunately, even the Hindu Trinity could not subdue Mahishasura. He continued wreaking havoc wherever he went.

Since only a woman could kill Mahishasura, Brahma, Vishnu and Shiva created a brilliant and powerful beam of energy from which Durga began to emerge. Indra and the other gods too sent out beams of energy. With Shiva's energy her face was formed, with Yama's energy the flowing hair. Her long and beautiful hands were formed with Vishnu's energy. The moon's energy created the breasts and Indra's the waist. Varun's energy shaped the upper and lower legs. Earth's energy formed the hips. Brahma created the feet, and Sun the toes. Kuber gave her a beautiful nose and the Prajapatis the teeth. Agni gave her three eyes, and others contributed brows, ears and other parts of the body. Thus was created a very beautiful woman, a divine goddess. Then the gods gave her beautiful clothes and a variety of jewels. A garland of pearls was placed around the neck. Each god had contributed the best to make the form most perfect. Looking at her, the gods experienced great joy.

Then each of the gods gave her their weapons. Vishnu gave his discus, Shiva gave her his trident, and Indra his thunderbolt. Agni presented a spear and Varun the conch. Vayu gave a bow with quivers that held an inexhaustible supply of arrows. Others gave the mace, the sword and shield and other weapons until her arsenal was complete. Airavata gave her a bell and Brahma a kamandal. Kuber gave her a pot of wine. The Sun gave her brilliance. Then the Himalayas gave her a lion as a vehicle. As she sat on the lion, her magnificence was dazzling. Experiencing her great might, she roared. Her voice reverberated through the hills and mountains, making them tremble. The trees shook as though in a storm. The waves in the sea rose to pound the shores. The gods looked at the Goddess with delight and awe and shouted, "Victory to Thee, O Mother!"

As the world reverberated with the challenge of the Goddess, everyone rushed out of their homes to see what had happened. Mahishasura was furious. Who was responsible for the commotion? The Asuras charged out to find the magnificent Goddess, seated on a lion, shining from head to toe. They lost no time in attacking her with all their weapons. The Goddess destroyed them with ease.

Mahishasura sent out the finest of his allies: warriors with chariots, elephants and horses, all armed with the best of weapons. But it was child's play for her. To make it more interesting, she created Ganas through her exhalation. The battlefield became crowded. The Ganas and the Asuras attacked each other. One could hear the shouting and shrieking over great distances. Blood flowed all around. The Asuras perished one by one along with their vast armies.

Mahishasura could tolerate this no longer. He took on the form of the wild buffalo and attacked the Ganas. He bellowed and kicked, felling many of them. He then turned towards the Goddess. He kicked up the earth in great fury in an attempt to frighten the lion. But the Goddess tied him in the pasa. He changed his form to that of a lion to confuse the Goddess. She cut off the lion's head. Mahishasura then took his real form and rushed at the Goddess with his sword. She felled him with an arrow. He then changed his form to that of an elephant and attacked the lion. The Goddess cut off his trunk. Once again, he took his real form.

The Goddess now thought it was time to end the battle. To lower Mahishasura's morale she pulled out her wine pot and drank out of it mockingly as he threw rocks at her. She turned the rocks to dust. Then jumping from the lion's back onto the buffalo's back, she pressed him

to the ground and pierced his neck with the trident. Mahishasura again changed to human form and attacked with a sword. Before he could change his form completely, the Goddess cut off his head, putting an end to him forever.

The moment Mahishasura fell, the gods led by Indra came, bowed in devotion and offered divine hymns in praise and salutation to the Goddess. They sang of her strength and valour. They praised her knowledge and wisdom. They extolled her numerous abilities and attributes. Above all, they conveyed how grateful they were for her benevolence. As a symbol of their gratitude, they offered her a garland made of the choicest flowers.

The Goddess then said, "I am pleased with your offerings and worship. Ask for any boon that you desire."

"Mother, you have fulfilled whatever we desired," the gods said. "If you so please, we only desire that in the future you protect us from harm before it overtakes us. We also desire that you bless those who are devoted and worship you, and make offerings as we have done, with happiness, prosperity and bliss."

"So be it," the Goddess said and left, changing her form once again.

Sumbha and Nisumbha

There is yet another legend in the **Devi Mahatmyam** of the **Markandey Purana** about the Asuras, Sumbha and Nisumbha. Both of them did not like the gods. They wanted to overcome them and rule the three worlds. To make it possible, they went to Pushkar and offered great sacrifices and penance to Brahma. Pleased by their devotion, Brahma granted them boons to fulfil their desires.

Armed with the boons, there was no stopping Sumbha and Nisumbha from achieving what they had set out for. Indra and the other gods felt helpless and quietly withdrew. Soon the gods realized that they could not possibly continue like this. They remembered that Goddess Durga had promised to help them whenever they would remember her. They got together, met Brahma, and with him proceeded to the Himalayas.

Together, the gods sang the hymn *Aparajita Stotra* in praise of the Goddess. This hymn pleases the Goddess. By her grace, the problems of all those who recite it are soon resolved.

Hearing this, Parvati appeared before the gods. It seemed as though she was going to the Ganga for a bath. "In whose praise are you singing this beautiful hymn?" she enquired.

Before the gods could explain their plight, a beautiful form emerged from Parvati's body and said, "They are calling out to me. Sumbha has turned them out of heaven and created terror in the three worlds." Since the Goddess came out of Parvati's body, she is also known as **Kousiki**. The Goddess shone in great brilliance as she stood before the gods. She said, "I will destroy the powerful Sumbha and Nisumbha." Then she proceeded towards the Himalayas. The gods felt relieved and returned to their homes.

The Goddess changed her form into that of a bewitchingly beautiful girl of sixteen and roamed about freely in gay abandon over the hills and mountains. Two of Sumbha's Asuras, Chanda and Munda, saw her. They were enchanted by her beauty, and could not take their eyes off her. They rushed to their master. "O Great King," they said, "we have never seen a more beautiful young woman. She is not a celestial nymph, nor is she one of us. She is like a thousand angels put together. We have seen her moving about alone. There is no one around her. It appears she is for a great king like you. Please bring her to the palace as your own."

On hearing Chanda and Munda, Sumbha desired to possess the girl. He summoned his trusted assistant Sugriva, and asked him to persuade her to become his queen.

When Sugriva met her, her beauty equally enchanted him. He said, "Madam, I am a messenger of the great King Sumbha, who rules over the three worlds. He desires that you become his queen. You have another choice. You could marry his younger brother Nisumbha, who is equally brave and powerful. There is nothing that the king does not possess. No one could give you greater pleasure."

The Goddess responded, "I believe what you have said. Sumbha and Nisumbha must be brave, having overtaken the three worlds. Inadvertently, I once took a vow that I would only marry the person who can humble me, or conquer me in battle. Therefore, if your king desires to marry me, he will have to defeat me, and then take me to his palace."

Sugriva was surprised by the counter proposal. "Madam, who can face the might of Sumbha and Nisumbha, rulers of the three worlds? How could a frail woman like you face them? I could personally take you to the king, pulling you by your tresses, but as a messenger, I resist from doing so. Please come with me."

"I might have made the vow without thinking of the consequences," the Goddess said, "but I am bound by it. Please tell your king about it."

Sugriva returned to Sumbha and narrated what had happened. Sumbha, in turn, summoned his trusted general Dhoomralochan, and asked him to bring the girl before him. If she resisted, he could bring her by pulling her tresses.

On meeting the Goddess, Dhoomralochan said, "Madam, please follow me to my king's palace. If you refuse, I will be compelled to take you there forcibly."

The Goddess smilingly said, "You look very brave and powerful. If you want to take me there forcibly, whatever can I do?"

As Dhoomralochan stepped forward to forcibly get hold of her, the Goddess uttered a terrible sound, "Hmmm." The vibration of the sound reduced the Asura to ashes. When the soldiers rushed to catch her, the Goddess's lion ran amok and killed them.

Sumbha was taken aback to hear what had happened. He then instructed Chanda and Munda to take a large force with them, kill the lion and bring the maiden to the palace. The forces rushed towards the Goddess. On seeing the unruly Asuras coming towards her, she was infuriated. Her face darkened with anger and her brows curled. From the angry face of the Goddess emerged the terrible form of **Kali**. Lean and thin almost like a skeleton, a very dark complexion with the eyes sunk in, the mouth wide open showing the canine teeth curving out and the restless thirsting tongue hanging out, she wore a tiger's skin and a garland of human skulls. She wielded a sword and a thick stick and carried a pasa. Emerging on the

ground she roared so loudly that the reverberations terrified everyone. She rushed towards the Asuras, their horses and elephants, crushing some under her feet, killing others and cutting off the heads of many. She gobbled many as though hungry for a long time.

Chanda and Munda charged at Kali when they saw their forces had been destroyed. She held Chanda's hair with one hand, and cut off his head with the other. She now attacked Munda. With a mighty blow of the stick, she felled Munda, and cut off his head. She picked up the two heads and placed them at the Goddess's feet. Pleased with what Kali had achieved, the Goddess said, "You have been victorious over both Chanda and Munda. You will forever be remembered as **Chamunda**."

Sumbha was extremely disturbed when he heard about the end of Chanda and Munda. He declared a state of emergency. All the Asuras were summoned with their forces to unitedly tackle the problem. Millions of Asura troops assembled in no time. They were led by mighty generals and moved towards the battlefield to attack the Goddess from all sides.

On seeing the vast Asura forces, the Goddess picked up her bow, pulled the string and let go, sending a resounding screeching sound that made everything shudder and tremble. Then she rang the bell just as the lion roared in unison. Kali roared the loudest of all, shaking the hills and mountains. The gods watched with joy. From each god emerged powers that they controlled, which merged with the Goddess. From Brahma emerged **Brahmani**, atop a swan, holding a kamandal and a garland of beads. From Shiva emerged **Maheshwari**, riding a bull, wielding a trident and adorning a crescent on the crown. Shiva also sent his trusted Virbhadra. From Kartikeya emerged **Kaumari**, riding a peacock and holding a spear. From Vishnu emerged **Vaishnavi**, seated on Garuda, and wielding the chakra, mace, bow and sword. **Varahi** and **Narasinhi** also emerged from Vishnu. From Indra emerged **Indrani** riding the elephant Airavata and wielding the Vajra.

Virbhadra bowed before the Goddess, and suggested that the Asuras may now be killed. Then a new form with great strength and speed emerged from the body of the Goddess. She was called **Chandika**. Numerous jackals surrounded her. She asked Virbhadra to serve as a messenger and to ask Sumbha and Nisumbha to return to their world. If they disagreed, use of force was the only option.

The Asuras were arrogant, and paid no heed. Without further delay, they attacked the Goddess. She was ready for them. Brahmani poured water from the kamandal on the Asuras. It rendered them powerless. The others attacked with their weapons, creating terror. Raktabeej, son of Sumbha's sister Krodhavati was asked to lead the attack. He was so blessed that every drop of his blood that fell on the ground would convert into an Asura of equal might and form. Raktabeej was huge and had a great store of blood within him. He confronted Indrani, but was wounded by her weapon Vajra. Vaishnavi, Kaumari and others attacked him, but as his blood flowed, innumerable Asuras emerged on the battlefield.

Then Chandika told Kali there was only one way to put an end to him. Kali should open her mouth and drink his blood, as Chandika attacked him with her weapons. In this way, together they were able to exhaust the blood in his body and Raktabeej was killed.

This further infuriated Sumbha and Nisumbha. They got together whatever forces were left and surrounded the Goddess on the battlefield. Nisumbha attacked first with a sword. She broke the sword and the shield. He then attacked her with a spear. Her discus cut it in midair. He tried his trident, the mace and the axe, but all his attacks were futile. However, the Goddess's arrows struck him and he fell unconscious.

Sumbha came forward. Kali enlarged her hands, and striking the skies created a terrible sound that reverberated throughout. Sumbha charged his spear with a mantra and hurled it at the Goddess. She countered it with a comet, destroying the spear. Sumbha lost his temper and roared with all his might. The Goddess felled him unconscious. By this time, Nisumbha regained consciousness and attacked. The Goddess pierced his chest with her trident. An Asura emerged from his chest, but she cut off his head with a sword. Thus the powerful Nisumbha was killed.

When Sumbha regained consciousness his anger knew no bounds on seeing what the Goddess had done. He shouted, "Durga, do not be proud of your strength. It is borrowed from others. Do not take it as your might and ability."

"Fool," the Goddess responded, "I am the only one. I control everything. See as I withdraw these powers back within me." The Goddess withdrew all the powers. She stood all by herself in the battlefield. "All that was mine has returned to me," she said. "Now be prepared to fight me."

Sumbha now used the divine weapons he had with him. None worked against the Goddess. He then tried to use his power to riddle her with arrows. In retaliation, she blew up Sumbha's chariot with horses and weapons, leaving him empty-handed. He then hit her on the chest.

She reciprocated, felling him unconscious. When he regained consciousness he grabbed the Goddess and jumped into the air. The two fought in the air endlessly. The Goddess held him by the hair and sent him crashing on the earth. He rose again with clenched fists to attack her. She pierced his chest with her trident and he fell down dead with a crashing sound, announcing that the world was free of the Asuras.

The gods came out of their hiding places. Prostrating in reverence before the Goddess, they sang hymns not only in her honour but also in honour of her many forms like Kali, Chandika, Narayani, Brahmani, Shivdooti, Maheshwari, Chamunda, Kaumari, Indrani and others. With all reverence to the Goddess, they conveyed their gratitude.

Pleased with gods, she said, "Do not hesitate to ask for whatever you desire. I will grant whatever you ask for."

The gods desired that whatever wrong was done should be corrected, so that they had no enemies. The Goddess agreed that whoever was devoted to her would find her with them. She would always reside in the homes where she was remembered every day.

The Changing Forms

A salient feature of Hindu thought is that individually, both man and woman are considered incomplete. Only when they unite in marriage are they considered complete. We have seen that just as the Hindu Trinity fulfils tasks on behalf of the Supreme Being, the three consorts equally complement those efforts and thereby fulfil their responsibilities. Even when it becomes necessary to go beyond the call of responsibility, everyone is ready to co-operate.

If Durga is the aggressive form of Parvati, her forms as Chandika and Chamunda are more violent. On an ascending scale of energy increase, Kali is the extreme form that knows no limits. While Kali is also described as Shiva's consort (extended form of Parvati), and the two are known to indulge unabashedly in the Tandava Nritya (a violent form of Shiva dance); in fact, Kali is usually depicted trampling Shiva. Such disrespect to the husband is not acceptable in Hindu thought, and the depiction is definitely not intended to portray Kali as being disrespectful to Shiva.

A positive interpretation would be that unbridled energy as we see in Kali can go out of control. To bring this energy — represented by Kali — under control, the only option open to Shiva was to lie down in her path, have her accidentally step on him, and — aghast at her error — regain control of her unbridled energy. This is why she is depicted biting her tongue in mortification at the indiscretion. Just as Shiva can be both benevolent and destructive, Parvati is equally capable of changing forms to Durga, Chandika and Kali. In times of need, she not only takes the support of Saraswati and Lakshmi, as Shakti of Brahma and Vishnu respectively, but also accesses the Shakti of Indra and other gods.

India is a vast country; with a widespread Hindu population comprising a multiplicity of languages and faiths, we find innumerable local goddesses known as Devi. In rural India, it is not uncommon for every village to have its own Devi, with a place of prayer assigned to her. She is credited (or discredited) for whatever happens in the village. Everyone tries to keep the Devi happy. Even in everyday life, pious Hindus consider young girls to be a form of Devi, piously offering them food and gifts at the end of the Navratri prayers.

Kali is often associated with the village or local patron goddess, or Devi. Here she is more often accepted in the form of a benevolent mother figure, rather than the aggressive form. Since a mother occupies an important status in Hinduism, it makes the role of many goddesses especially significant.

Kali is derived from the word *kala*, which means *time*. She is therefore often represented as one who devours time, and is symbolic of death. Since the word *kala* also refers to the colour black, Kali can also mean a dark complexioned woman. As symbolic of life energy, Kali also means *breath*. As long as one breathes, one is alive. Hence, her association with timelessness and breath can also be interpreted as one who confers immortality, beyond the pale of death.

Worship of Durga, Kali and other Goddesses

While there are temples devoted to various goddesses in most villages, in bigger towns and cities there are temples dedicated mostly to Durga. There are few that are dedicated to Kali. During the Navratri, thousands of temporary pandals (tent structures) are erected to house the idols of the goddesses and other deities. At the end of the festivities, the idols are immersed in rivers or the sea.

An important shrine dedicated to **Vaishno Devi**, also known as **Mata Rani**, is situated near Katra, in Jammu and Kashmir. Hundreds of thousands of devotees visit this shrine from all parts of the country every year. The shrine is in a holy cave where Vaishno Devi killed

Bhairon Nath, who did not want her to attain spirituality. He desired that she should marry him. At the moment of death, it is said that Bhairon Nath uttered her name and gained salvation, and many now observe the custom of praying first at his shrine before proceeding to the Devi's temple. It is believed that Vaishno Devi assumed the shape of a rock with three heads, and went into perpetual meditation.

In adjoining Himachal Pradesh, there are shrines dedicated to **Kangrawali Devi**, **Chintpurni**, and **Jwalaji** where the Devi is manifested as a perpetual flame. Devotees visit these shrines all round the year. Similarly, there are shrines dedicated to **Chandika**, **Chamunda**, **Meenakshi**, **Mansa**, **Shakumbri**, **Renuka**, **Naina**, **Santoshi** and many more in various parts of the country. They are all considered to be benevolent to their devotees.

Worship of Shakti

Just as Vaishnavites consider Vishnu the Supreme Being, Shaivites look up to Shiva and Shakts consider Shakti — or the female energy form — as the highest one. However, this is purely of academic interest; few Hindus are rigid in their beliefs. The majority is flexible, and depending upon personal upbringing, beliefs and experiences, they accept and pray to one or more gods and goddesses.

Sri Ram

Sri Ram is the seventh incarnation of Vishnu. In terms of worship, he is perhaps the most important incarnation of Vishnu. Worship to him is not restricted to temples alone. Each year, his exemplary life is re-enacted in the form of Ram Lila, with young boys and girls playing the key roles in the drama that lasts one to two weeks, culminating with the death of Ravan on Dussehra day, and Sri Ram's coronation the following day.

Groups of villages, smaller towns, cities and the metros are simultaneously involved, each group putting on as good a show as their abilities and budgets allow. Thousands of such groups operate simultaneously during the Navratri each year. Children take great delight in playing with bows and arrows, swords and maces and wearing a variety of masks that craftsmen make in time for the celebrations.

Television replays of the ever-popular serials on the Ramayan keep families glued to the television sets, further reinforcing the belief in Sri Ram. People have watched the life of Sri Ram being enacted in the Ram Lila and in television serials, ever since childhood, yet they never seem to have enough of it. The enthusiasm and inspiration compels people to watch this again and again. Thus, even after thousands of years, Sri Ram continues to influence millions of people around the world.

The Ramayan

The Ramayan is the story of Sri Ram. *Ramayan,* in Sanskrit, literally means *the journey of Ram.* The sage Valmiki originally wrote it in Sanskrit. Of the two Hindu epics, the Ramayan and the Mahabharat, the Ramayan came earlier. It is almost 5000 years old. The Mahabharat came later, and contains references to the Ramayan as do the Vishnu Purana and the Vayu Purana. The Adhyatma Ramayan in Sanskrit is a shortened version of the epic.

Several versions of the Ramayan followed. Sant Tulsi Das gave a Hindi version in poetic form as the Ramcharitmanas. This version is extremely popular. Millions of copies have gone into Hindu homes. Kamban, a Tamil poet, named his version as Kambaramayanam. A Kannada version by Dr K.V. Puttappa is called Shri Ramayana Darshanam. Vishwanath Satyanarayan's Telegu version is entitled Ramayana Kalpavrikshamu. Eminent writers and thinkers have made many translations of the Ramayan in both English poetry and prose.

The Ramayan is equally popular — in different forms and languages — in South East Asian countries. The Kakawin Ramayan of Java, Indonesia, Hikayat Seri Ram of Malaysia, Ramakein of Thailand, the Ramakavaca of Bali, Yama Zatdaw of Myanmar, the Reamker of Cambodia, Pra Lak Pra Lam of Laos and Maradia Lawana of the Philippines are unique versions of the Ramayan where the authors have incorporated local history, folklore and religious beliefs to make the epic relevant to that particular region.

Maryada Purushottam Ram

The word *Purushottam* simply means the *best amongst men*. The epithet *Maryada Purushottam* would thus mean *an outstanding man*, or *the perfect man*, who has the attributes of self-control and good behaviour. It means one who is a leader amongst men, one who knows how to face all kinds of situations.

The Perfect Man

If Sri Ram was born as a human being to establish good over evil, it is significant that despite being born as a prince in a royal household, his life was marked by simplicity and concern for others. Sri Ram was an ideal son, an ideal student, an ideal brother, an ideal master and an ideal king. Everyone adored him.

When Sri Ram and Ravan came face to face for the first time, Sri Ram stepped forward and with folded hands said, "I bow to you, O Master of the Vedas."

Ravan retorted, "Are you already afraid to face me in battle?"

Sri Ram responded, "You are a Brahmin. You are wise and knowledgeable. Courtesy requires that I

respect you for your abilities. We have come to the battlefield for a purpose. We will fulfil that too."

That evening, speaking to his wife Mandodari, Ravan said, "My opponent in battle is an expert in archery. But he speaks even more convincingly. His words touch the heart."

Sri Ram and Shabari

When Sri Ram met Sabari in the forest, she led him to her hut. All she had were berries picked from bushes in the forest. She offered these to him, after making sure they were not sour. She confessed that she was an ignorant woman, an outcaste, and the only evidence of devotion she had was a broom with which she cleared the pathway so that her Lord could reach the hut without discomfort.

Sri Ram was moved by her devotion, "Good lady, I recognise nothing but a person's devotion. Everything else is secondary. A person without devotion is like a cloud without water." He continued thoughtfully, "There are nine kinds of devotion. The first is companionship of saints. The second is when people take interest in stories about me. The third is service to the guru. The fourth consists in singing my praises. The chanting of the name with faith is the fifth kind of devotion. The sixth includes the practice of self-control and virtue. The seventh kind sees me in everything, accepting saints as part of me. The eighth aims at remaining content and not finding fault with others. The ninth requires that one should be honest and sincere in dealing with everyone, with faith in me. Whoever possesses any of the nine kinds of devotion is dear to me, irrespective of whether the devotee is a man, a woman or an animal. Good lady, you are endowed with all kinds of devotion."

In the **Ramcharitmanas,** Aranya-kand, Doha 36, it is said:
Sri Ram blessed Shabari with salvation. She was not only an outcaste, but also a sinner. Fool, you seek happiness, not remembering the Master?

A Lesson for Vibhishan

In another situation, when Sri Ram and Ravan came face to face in battle, Vibhishan saw that while Sri Ram stood on the ground, Ravan was in a shining chariot with a charioteer. The chariot was equipped with many powerful weapons. Vibhishan felt that it was an unequal fight. He went up to Sri Ram and said, "My Lord, Ravan is on a well-equipped chariot. You have no chariot. You have no armour, nor any other kind of protection. Does this not make it difficult to conquer this great warrior?"

Sri Ram smilingly responded, "Friend, the chariot that carries one to victory is different from the one you see. Courage and valour are its two wheels. Truth and good behaviour are its flag and banner. Strength, discretion, self-control and benevolence are the four horses. These horses are joined to the chariot with compassion, forgiveness and a balanced mind. Devotion to god is the charioteer. Impartiality is the shield and contentment is the sword. Charity is the axe, reasoning the lance and wisdom the bow. A clear mind is the quiver and religious observances are the arrows. Respect for the guru and for Brahmins serves as the coat of mail. One who has such a chariot will have no enemies to conquer. One with such a chariot can conquer even the most difficult of enemies — attachment to materialistic pleasures."

In the **Ramcharitmanas,** Lanka-kand, Doha 80A, it is said:
Whoever possesses these intrinsic qualities can conquer even the most invincible of enemies — attachment to the world!

The Good and the Wicked

After Sri Ram became the king of Ayodhya, he would spend every afternoon with his brothers, gurus and others discussing the Vedas, Puranas and the truths of everyday life. Bharat once hesitantly asked Sri Ram, "Lord, you are most kind. The Vedas and the Puranas sing the glory of the saints and the sages. You too have always given them great respect and honour. Could you tell me about the traits of the good and the wicked?"

"Brother, the Vedas and Puranas describe many characteristics of saints," Sri Ram explained. "The saints and the wicked can be compared to sandalwood and the axe. The axe cuts down the sandalwood tree, but the sandalwood in return imparts its fragrance to the axe. The sandalwood is rubbed and its paste is applied on the forehead of the gods. Everyone loves the fragrance and the coolness of the sandalwood paste. The axe gets blunt and is thrown into the fire to make it red hot and then beaten with a hammer to make it sharp once again."

As the three brothers and Hanuman heard Sri Ram with rapt attention, he continued, "Saints are a storehouse of virtues. They are beyond mere sensual pleasure. They are considerate about others, rejoice at others' success, and grieve at their distress. They are free from passion and vanity. They have conquered greed, anger and fear. They have control over their mind and senses, are calm and patient, always behave well and never use a harsh word. Praise and criticism are alike for them. Such people are dear to me."

As Sri Ram paused, Bharat said, "What about the wicked?"

"The wicked must always be avoided," Sri Ram continued. "Their company brings unhappiness. The wicked are forever burning with jealousy. The prosperity of others pains them. They are delighted at others' loss. They love no one. They speak lies as though it were the truth. Their speech is sweet like honey, but their heart is like that of a snake, ready to hurt everyone. They have an evil eye for others' women and wealth. These sinful men are really demons disguised as human beings. They are greedy for everything — food, wealth and sexual enjoyment. Selfish as they are, they have no respect for father, mother, guru or Brahmins, and are quick to antagonize others. They may look saintly, but are deceitful hypocrites."

The **Ramcharitmanas,** Uttar-kand, Doha 38, states:
Sri Ram said, "Those who are devoted to me and accept praise and criticism equally are dear to me. Such people are virtuous and embodiments of bliss."

Sri Ram was loved by his gurus Vasishtha and Vamadev, by his mothers, brothers and the citizens of Ayodhya. If Sri Ram gave respect to sages and saints, they reciprocated it with love. The life of Sri Ram was one that spreads joy, happiness and bliss even today.

Ram Rajya

An important achievement of Sri Ram was that after he put an end to the demons, he established Ram Rajya — a state of good governance. The **Ramayan** describes it thus:

"The people cared for each other. Each fulfilled the duty entrusted to him. Every man loved his wife and children. Every woman was faithful to her husband and sincerely cared for the family. The elderly and the wise were respected. There was righteousness everywhere. Life was based on the four pillars of righteousness — truth, purity, compassion and charity. There was no suffering, nor sickness. There were no calamities. No one was destitute or miserable. All were good, pious and virtuous. Learning and wisdom prevailed. Everyone lived an honest life.

"Sri Ram was revered as the undisputed sovereign. Everyone sought his guidance. By talking about him and hearing of his exploits, everyone desired to learn about his infinite greatness. It was difficult to describe the joy and happiness of the people. The land gave abundant crops. The trees flowered and bore fruit. Even the animals regarded each other as friends. The mountains were rich in minerals and gems. The rivers gave clean water. The seas swept the shores with valuable jewels for all.

"Ayodhya was an important destination for all sages and saints. The city was more attractive than Indra's Amravati. Each house was beautiful. Gardens and parks were full of flowers and fruits. Nature was bountiful. The bees hummed while the birds fluttered from tree to tree, enjoying their beauty. The fields yielded sufficient grain for everyone. The markets were full of goods. The people were happy and content. Everyone adored Sri Ram."

Sri Ram and Sita

If Sri Ram was an embodiment of beauty, charm and virtue, his efforts were perfectly complemented by his wife Sita. She supported her lord in every way. There were enough servants to look after the needs of the palaces, but she insisted on looking after Sri Ram and the mothers personally, much to their delight.

Sita was an incarnation of Lakshmi, and despite the hardships of life in the forest she insisted upon being with Sri Ram during the fourteen years in exile. When Sri Ram, Sita and Lakshman were leaving Chitrakut to proceed to Panchvati, they visited the sage Atri and his wife Anasuya.

In the **Ramcharitmanas,** Aranya-kand, Dohas 5A and B, Anasuya tells Sita:

A woman is incomplete at birth. She becomes complete and attains happiness through union with a husband. It is for her devotion to her husband that the Lord loved Tulsi. The four Vedas sing of her glory. Sita, by invoking your blessings, women will be faithful to their husbands. I speak to you for the welfare of mankind."

Despite Sita's great devotion, on hearing of the public censure, Sri Ram was compelled to send her to live in Valmiki's hermitage in the forest. At that time, she was expecting the Lord's successor. Many ardent devotees of Sri Ram feel that it was wrong of him to have forsaken Sita, especially since she had earlier been tested through Agni Pariksha.

Sita was devastated when Lakshman explained the purpose of their visit to the forest. Taking control of her emotions, as Lakshman prepared to leave, she said, "Lakshman, on your return home, courteously convey my regards to my mothers-in-law. Enquire about the welfare of the Lord. With respect and downcast head, convey my message: "Lord, you know that I am pure and devoted, and concerned about your welfare. You have forsaken me due to fear of infamy. I would not like you to be censured. I prefer to be forsaken rather than have infamy fall upon you. Always treat the citizens like your brothers. Impartiality and good behaviour will create goodwill. Just as it is necessary for a king to keep public criticism in mind, it is equally important for the wife to fulfil her responsibility towards the husband. A wife should not hesitate to do this, even at the cost of her life."

Worship of Sri Ram

Temples dedicated to Sri Ram can be seen everywhere. He is shown sitting or standing with Sita on his left, and Lakshman, ready to serve, always standing on his right. Hanuman is shown kneeling at his feet, ever the ardent devotee. Almost every Hindu home has images of Sri Ram.

Many read the Ramayan as a part of their prayers. It is considered auspicious to read the Ramayan uninterrupted on special occasions. A team reads it with many joining, singing the verses together to the accompaniment of a musical instrument. It takes 24 hours to read the entire text.

Worship of Sri Ram reaches its highest pitch during Navratri when the Ram Lila is enacted in villages, towns and cities. It reminds everyone that righteousness always overcomes evil. At Dussehra when the effigies of Meghnad, Kumbhkaran and Ravan are consigned to the flames amidst great joy, there is only one call: "Glory to Sri Ram."

There is magic in the name of Sri Ram. It carries one through the most difficult of situations. Bharat ruled Ayodhya for fourteen years by placing Sri Ram's *padukas* (wooden sandals) on the throne, and seeking their guidance. Hanuman had Sri Ram and Sita enshrined within his heart.

In the **Skand Purana,** Lord Shiva tells Parvati:

'*Ram Naam*' — *chanting the two-syllable mantra absolves one of all sins. Whoever chants* '*Ram Naam*' *when moving, sitting or sleeping, or whenever possible, finds fulfilment and, eventually, a place with Sri Hari.*

Even when Hindus die, the dead body is carried to the crematorium with the chanting of: '*Ram naam satya hai*' — meaning *the name of Sri Ram is the ultimate truth*. It is believed that the chanting entitles the deceased to a place in Vaikunth.

13

Hanuman

Hanuman

Hanuman met Sri Ram and Lakshman when they were looking for Sita, who had been abducted by Ravan. Hanuman introduced Sri Ram and Lakshman to Sugriva. The friendship that blossomed helped Sugriva become king of Kiskindha. In turn, Sugriva's associates helped locate Sita in Lanka. She was rescued and brought back after Sri Ram, supported by Sugriva's forces, killed Ravan and his demon associates.

Punjikasthala, an apsara, was once cursed and reborn as a female *vanara*, Anjana. She was married to Kesari, a powerful *vanara*, who once killed an elephant creating problems for saints and sages in the forest. Together they prayed to Shiva that they might have a son like him. Pleased by their devotion, Shiva agreed to be born as their son. Anjana met Vayu, the Wind God, and Hanuman was born. Hanuman is known by several names. As the son of Vayu or Pavan, he is known as **Pavanputra** and **Maruti**. As the son of Kesari and Anjana, he is also known as **Kesarinandan** and **Anjaneya**. He is often addressed by using the prefix *Sankatmochan*, meaning *one who liberates from crises*.

Hanuman's Childhood

On one occasion when Indra hurt Hanuman during his childhood, Vayu took him to Patal Lok. In Vayu's absence, everyone started gasping for breath. Indra and the other gods rushed to seek Vayu's pardon. To please him, they showered many boons on Hanuman. Above all, they granted him immortality.

Hanuman is virtuous, loyal, powerful and courageous. He is knowledgeable, righteous and dutiful. Like his father, he can fly at great speed and reach his destination quickly. Surya was his teacher and taught him all that he knew. Despite his qualities, as a child Hanuman was naughty and teased sages when they were in meditation. Irritated by his pranks, they cursed him that, unless reminded, he would not remember his might. Hanuman is humble and easily pleased. Due to the curse, he is forgetful. He needs to be repeatedly reminded of his strength and prowess.

Sunderkand

Hanuman is described as the greatest devotee of Sri Ram. You will find him wherever there is a temple dedicated to Sri Ram. Hanuman played a crucial

role in tracing Sita's whereabouts. The details are described in **Sunderkand**, the fifth part of the **Ramayan**.

Sunderkand is a beautiful, rhythmic, verbal description. Of the 60 couplets, the first 30 pertain to the description and character of Hanuman, and the rest to the qualities of Sri Ram. The word *sunder* (meaning *beautiful*, *handsome*, *virtuous*, and *good*) appears in 24 *chaupais*. Hanuman is the chief character in Sunderkand. Within Sunderkand there are several stories. These help the mentally disturbed to achieve peace and harmony.

Sunderkand gives a vivid description of Hanuman's abilities, and his strength, knowledge and wisdom. With the blessings of Sri Ram, he is able to cross the ocean in a single leap. When challenged by Lankini, guarding the gates to Lanka, he overcomes her and gains entrance. He is able to locate Vibhishan's house. On meeting Vibhishan, he is able to win him over by causing dissension.

When he meets Sita in the Ashok Vatika, her plight distresses him deeply. Though he is a bachelor, Hanuman is able to convey an emotionally charged description of Sri Ram's longing for her. On hearing it, Sita forgets her own pangs of her separation from her husband. Hanuman challenges the Ashok Vatika guards and kills Ravan's son. To reach Ravan, he intentionally falls into Meghnad's trap.

On meeting Ravan, he uses a policy of simplicity and mildness. He behaves as though he is an ordinary monkey. At the same time, he explains to Ravan how he could win the favour of Sri Ram. When he is punished by having his tail set on fire, he takes advantage of the situation by leaping about and burning down a major part of Lanka, striking terror into the hearts of its citizens. After obtaining Sita's blessings, he returns to Sri Ram to unburden him from the longing of separation from Sita. He motivates Sri Ram to prepare for war. When Sri Ram praises Hanuman and tells him that he has incurred a debt he can never repay, much to everyone's surprise, Hanuman holds Sri Ram's feet saying, "Save me! Save me, my Lord! Please do not let me fall a victim to pride."

Besides the beauty and the inspiration of the verses, Sunderkand leads one towards the attainment of spiritual knowledge.

Aversion to Pride

Hanuman is averse to pride. One such instance is described in the **Mahabharat**. In his old age, when he was sitting in a quiet spot in the forest praying, Bhim, his half brother, son of Vayu and Kunti,

tripped over his tail. Bhim complained why the old monkey could not look after his tail. Hanuman said he was too old, and asked Bhim if he could help move it out of the way. When Bhim, always proud of his strength, tried to lift the tail, he could not move it at all. Thus did Hanuman destroy the pride of his half brother.

On another occasion, Hanuman humbled the pride of Shani, who thought he could create problems for anyone. Hanuman effortlessly gripped Shani tightly with his tail. Hanuman let him off only when Shani promised that he would never create problems for devotees of Sri Ram.

Hanuman and Lakshman

During the war with Meghnad, Ravan's favourite son, when Lakshman was gravely wounded, Hanuman played another crucial role to end the crisis. With no physician to attend to Lakshman, Hanuman transported Susena, house and all, from Lanka. When Susena said that the only remedy was the Sanjivini herb, and it must be brought before dawn, Hanuman flew thousands of miles north to get it. Unable to identify the herb, Hanuman picked up Mount Dronagiri and brought it back for Susena to locate the herb.

Hanuman and Mahiravan

On another occasion when Mahiravan, a practitioner of black magic, captured Sri Ram and Lakshman and carried them to Patal Lok, Hanuman went there but learnt that only a person who could extinguish five lamps simultaneously could kill Mahiravan. Hanuman assumed the *Panchmukha* (five-faced) form, extinguished the five lamps and killed Mahiravan to rescue Sri Ram and Lakshman.

Worship of Hanuman

When Sri Ram left for Vaikunth after completing the responsibilities of his incarnation, many of his colleagues went with him, but Hanuman stayed back. He wished to ensure that Sri Ram was remembered forever. It is said that several saints like Tulsidas and Ramdas Swami have seen Hanuman.

Hanuman temples are to be found not only all over India where the majority of Hindus live, but in many other countries. An 85-foot-high idol of Hanuman (known as *Karya Siddhi* Hanuman) is the pride of Carapichaima in Trinidad and Tobago. Wherever there is a temple devoted to Sri Ram, Hanuman is always there, kneeling on one side, or standing behind him. In temples where Hanuman is the principal deity, he is coated with vermilion. When prayers are offered, it is customary for the priest to put a dot of vermilion on the devotee's forehead as a blessing. The use of vermilion can be traced back to the Ramayan.

One morning when Hanuman went to Sita, on seeing the vermilion in the parting on her head, he enquired, "Mother, what red colour do you have in the parting of your hair?" Sita responded smilingly, "Son, this is *sindoor* (vermilion). It is symbolic of a married woman, and is auspicious for a happy married life. A woman seeking her husband's longevity, applies it throughout her life. It is symbolic of the husband's contentment."

Hanuman wondered that if a pinch of vermilion ensured a long life for the master, would applying it on his entire body not make his master immortal? 'Yes, it would,' he thought. He applied vermilion all over his body and went to Sri Ram's court. Everybody in the assembly laughed. This embarrassed Hanuman. Sri Ram also smiled at what Hanuman had done, but chose not to laugh at his show of devotion. Sri Ram knew Hanuman was humble, simple-hearted and obsessed with devotion for his master, so he said, "Whoever offers vermilion and oil to my dearest Hanuman shall always be dear to me. Such people shall receive my blessings. All their desires will be fulfilled."

Hanuman was pleased with his master's response. He thought of what Sita had told him. After Sri Ram's blessings, Hanuman's faith in Sita's advice became stronger. Since the intimate relationship between Sri Ram and Hanuman is remembered by offering vermilion dissolved in oil to Hanuman, the ceremony of coating Hanuman's idol with vermilion is literally called 'offering clothes to Hanuman'.

Devotees pray to Hanuman by reading the *Hanuman Chalisa* (40 verses of praise) every day. Those who can spare more time read the **Sunderkand**. Through it, they seek the favours of Hanuman. It is believed that by chanting the Sunderkand regularly, one can overcome poverty and sorrow. All obstacles and hurdles are easily overcome. Householders are blessed with success and happiness.

During the Mahabharat, Hanuman was eager to serve yet another incarnation of Vishnu. He attached himself to the flag of Arjun's chariot. This enabled him to hear the **Bhagavad Gita** first hand as Sri Krishna addressed Arjun.

Hanuman is the solace for all those facing a crisis. He is truly *Sankatmochan* — he who protects everyone from crises. Hundreds of thousands of devotees line up every Tuesday and Saturday at Hanuman temples to seek relief from their problems.

14

Sri Krishna

Sri Krishna

Sri Krishna is the eighth incarnation of Vishnu and is considered to be the most complete one. Like Sri Ram, Sri Krishna is widely worshipped by Hindus around the world. Of the four Dhams, two of them, the Jagannath temple at Puri and the other at Dwarka, are dedicated to Sri Krishna. Magnificent temples dedicated to him are spread all over the world.

Though not of the same magnitude, the *Krishna Lila*, or *Ras Lila*, is also organized on the same pattern as the *Ram Lila*. Television serials and films on the life and exploits of Sri Krishna are as popular as those on  the life of Sri Ram. Like Sri Ram, Sri Krishna too has influenced the lives of millions of people.

With organisations like the International Society for Krishna Consciousness (ISKCON), the glory of Sri Krishna has spread beyond the boundaries of India, and many are not only embracing Hinduism, but also obtaining solace from their devotion to this deity.

The earliest references to Sri Krishna are to be found in the epic **Mahabharat** by Ved Vyas. The **Harivamsa** followed the Mahabharat. More detailed accounts are available in the **Bhagavata Purana** and the **Vishnu Purana**. The most significant part of the Mahabharat is the Bhishma Parv that constitutes the **Bhagavad Gita**, wherein Sri Krishna advises Arjun on the eternal truths of life. Translated into many languages, the Bhagavad Gita is read by millions of people — Hindus and non-Hindus alike. It is an eternal source of wisdom and inspiration to all Hindus.

Sri Krishna

In Sanskrit, the word *Krishna* literally means *black,* or *the dark one.* This refers to Sri Krishna's complexion, similar to that of Vishnu and Sri Ram — dark and bluish-black. The deities are also shown with a dark complexion. In the Mahabharat, the meaning of Krishna is explained as one who is symbolic of the *Absolute Truth.* Others have interpreted it to mean *a union of existence and bliss* and *storehouse of great joy.*

Of the 1008 names of Vishnu, many are linked with Sri Krishna. **Jagannath** means the lord of the universe; **Gopal** — one who protects the cows; **Vasudeva** — the son of Vasudev; **Keshav** — one who has long hair; **Madhav** — the husband of the goddess of fortune; **Hrishikesh** — the lord of the senses. Devotees use any of the names that make them happy.

The Birth of Sri Krishna

The purpose of this incarnation of Vishnu was to end the atrocities being committed against the righteous. At the time of Sri Krishna's birth, Kans was ruler of Mathura. Ruthless and brutal, in his lust for power he had imprisoned his own father, King Ugrasen, and usurped the throne. Since he was forewarned that his sister's eighth son would kill him, he imprisoned her along with her husband. Each time they were blessed with a son, he would kill him. Since they were in a well-guarded prison, no one could help them.

Sri Krishna was the eighth son born to Devki, and her husband Vasudev, in a dark prison cell in Mathura. It was raining torrentially. The river Yamuna flowing nearby was flooded. That night as the guards slept, the prison doors opened miraculously, the flooding river subsided and Vasudev carried the baby across the river, to leave him safely with foster parents Nand

and Yashoda in Gokul. In exchange, he brought back a newly born baby girl. The next morning, despite sister Devki's pleas, Kans killed the baby girl. However, he felt that there was something mysterious going on, and with the fear of Devki's eighth son tormenting his mind, he did not want to take any chances.

Sri Krishna's Childhood

To ensure he was not cheated, Kans set out to kill all the baby boys born around that time. His spies traced Sri Krishna and his half-brother Balram to the home of Nand and Yashoda. Kans made several attempts to kill Sri Krishna and Balram through his henchmen. However, in the effort, demons like Putna, Shakt, Trinavart, Agh, Keshi and several others lost their lives.

Sri Krishna's childhood was spent with boys and girls looking after cows. The boys led by Sri Krishna played a lot of pranks, stealing the butter from *gopis* (girls who reared cows), and teasing them as they bathed in the river Yamuna. Sri Krishna enthralled not only the boys and girls, but also the cows and other animals when he played the flute. It seemed like Goddess Saraswati was playing it. Everyone would thirst for more.

During his childhood, much to the astonishment and horror of everyone, Sri Krishna jumped into the Yamuna to punish Kaliya Nag who was polluting the river, making the water unfit for use. On another occasion he picked up the Govardhan hill on his little finger so that people could find shelter under it until the torrential rains sent down by Indra stopped.

The education of Sri Krishna and Balram was entrusted to the sage Sandipani. When it was time to give *guru dakshina* (the teacher's fee), the sage demanded that Sri Krishna and Balram bring back his son to him. The son had been abducted by a demon, Panchjanya. They were able to locate the demon through information from Varun, the Sea God. They killed the demon, and got the son back from Yama, the God of Death, thus pleasing the guru.

The Death of Kans

Kans continued to be obsessed by the fear of Devki's eighth son, and had his eyes set on Sri Krishna and Balram. Once again, plotting to kill them, he organized a wrestling match for them. Not only did the two brothers win, Sri Krishna now felt it was time for Kans to die. He killed him amidst the vast audience that had assembled for the wrestling match. King Ugrasen was freed and installed as king once again. Devki and Vasudev were also released from prison. By now they had a daughter, a younger sister of Sri Krishna and Balram. Peace returned to Mathura.

But all was not well for Sri Krishna. With the death of Kans, Sri Krishna had a new enemy in Jarasandh, two of whose daughters were married to Kans. He repeatedly attacked Mathura, but Sri Krishna and Balram kept repelling the attacks. However, Jarasandh was determined. He continued to attack Mathura. Fighting was an expensive activity, so Sri Krishna thought it wiser to leave with the other Yadavs, and settle down to build a new kingdom in Dwarka. This gave Sri Krishna a new name — **Ranchhod,** meaning *one who has run away from the battlefield.* Despite loss of reputation, Sri Krishna felt it was in everyone's interest to give up an attitude of confrontation.

Sri Krishna's Family

Sri Krishna had 16,008 wives. The eight principal wives were Rukmini, Jambvati, Kalindi, Satyabhama, Mitravinda, Satya, Lakshmana and Bhadra.

He married the other 16,000 to give them protection after he saved them from the clutches of the demon Narkasura, son of the demon, Hiranyaksh and Bhumi, to whom Vishnu had given a weapon at Bhumi's request. This weapon carried with it the blessing that no one could kill Narkasura as long as he had the weapon with him. This boon made the demon arrogant and he created terror everywhere. He even threatened Indra, the King of Gods. He held 16,000 damsels captive. At the request of the gods, Sri Krishna attacked Narkasura, killing him and his associates. Since the 16,000 damsels had nowhere to go, Sri Krishna took them as his wives and sent them to Dwarka, where he built a special palace for them.

The Mahabharat

The Mahabharat describes of the lives of the Pandavas and the Kauravas, and the battle that followed when the two rival groups could not come to an understanding. The role of Sri Krishna is significant as he was well connected with both groups, and even made efforts to resolve differences between them.

Besides Dev Vrat — more popularly known as Bhishma Pitamah, son of Shantanu and Ganga — Shantanu, the King of Hastinapur, had two other sons: Chitrangad and Vichitravirya. Dev Vrat had vowed never to marry or become king. Chitrangad died, and Vichitravirya became king. He begot two sons: Pandu, and Dhritrashtra, who was blind from birth. Pandu had two wives: Kunti and Madri. Pandu had retired to the forest with them, where they gave birth to five sons, known as Pandavas. Dhritrashtra, who served as king, begot a hundred sons

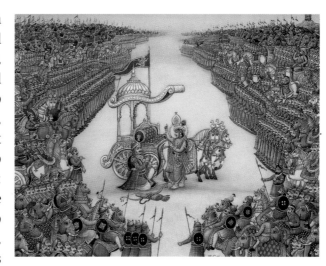

through his wife, Gandhari. They were known as Kauravas. When Pandu and Madri died, Kunti returned to Hastinapur with the Pandavas.

The Pandavas and the Kauravas grew up together, learning the Vedas and the art of using a variety of weapons. Since the Pandavas proved to be superior, the Kauravas were jealous of them. With their father as king, they always took advantage of their position. Bhishma brought the situation under control by dividing the kingdom. He decided that the Kauravas would rule from Hastinapur, and the Pandavas from Indraprasth. However, this peace was short-lived. The Kauravas were always conspiring for a showdown with the Pandavas, to usurp whatever they had. Taking advantage of the Pandavas' weakness for gambling, the Kauravas not only cheated and defeated them in a game of dice, but also insulted them and their wife Draupadi, and sent them into a thirteen-year exile, twelve of these in the forest, and one year incognito.

When the Pandavas returned after thirteen years, the Kauravas were still not willing to give anything to the Pandavas. All attempts at compromise having failed, the Pandavas were left with no other choice but to resolve the issue through war that came to be known as Mahabharat.

Role of Sri Krishna

The battlelines had already been drawn the day the Kauravas cheated the Pandavas in a game of dice, and Duryodhan, the eldest of the Kauravas, asked his younger brother Duhshasan to drag Draupadi to the court by her hair. While King Dhritrashtra and all the elders sat in the court as mute spectators, Duryodhan asked Duhshasan to pull off Draupadi's sari in open court. The Pandavas sat helpless and ashamed. Draupadi knew only Sri Krishna could help her, so she called out in prayer to him. Her prayer was answered: no matter for how long Duhshasan kept unwrapping the sari, it would not end. The exhausted Duhshasan finally gave up. Sri Krishna thus helped protect Draupadi's modesty and self-respect. That day, she vowed that she would leave her hair open until the day Duryodhan and Duhshasan were punished. This took place at the end of the Mahabharat.

Sri Krishna knew both the groups well, and travelled from Dwarka to Hastinapur to negotiate peace. Sri Krishna was a hard negotiator, and sought that the five brothers be given five villages. But the Kauravas arrogantly insisted that they could not give land even the size of the head of a needle. Sri Krishna therefore returned to Dwarka.

Both the Pandavas and the Kauravas then garnered support for the war. Sri Krishna had his forces, and obviously both would seek his support. Duryodhan went on behalf of the Kauravas, and Arjun for the Pandavas. When Duryodhan arrived at the palace, Sri Krishna was sleeping. He sat by his head, waiting for Sri Krishna to wake up. Arjun arrived a little later, and sat by Sri Krishna's feet. When Sri Krishna woke up he found both waiting, seeking his support. Sri Krishna said that he respected both groups. To be fair, his forces would be on

one side, and he alone would be on the other. Furthermore, he would not carry a weapon or personally fight. Since he had seen Arjun first on waking up, he let Arjun have the first choice. Arjun chose Sri Krishna.

Duryodhan had come only to seek the forces, and was happy to get what he wanted. Sri Krishna decided to be the *sarthi* (charioteer) of Arjun's chariot.

When the battle between the Pandavas and the Kauravas began, and Sri Krishna drove Arjun's chariot through the battle lines, Arjun felt discouraged. On both sides stood his own kith and kin, all of those who were dear to him, ready to kill each other. He asked himself, 'What will I gain by killing my own people? Whether I win, or I lose, either way I would be the loser.' Seeing Arjun torn by doubt, Sri Krishna spoke to him on the duties and responsibilities of humankind, and how these can be fulfilled. This dialogue is known as the **Bhagavad Gita**.

In the 700 verses divided into 18 chapters, this timeless dialogue between Sri Krishna and Arjun is as valid today as it was thousands of years ago when it took place. The **Bhagavad Gita**, the most widely read scripture of the Hindus, is dear even to non-Hindus for the practical philosophy of life that it expounds. In the course of his dialogue Sri Krishna disclosed his divine form to a stunned Arjun.

The Mahabharat war lasted just seventeen days. All of the 100 sons of Dhritrashtra and Gandhari were killed, and so were the elders. The Pandavas too lost many young lives, but the five brothers survived. The moves made by the two factions cannot be described as righteous, but Sri Krishna, as an incarnation, looked at the results, and not the means used to achieve them. When Sri Krishna met Gandhari, the mother of the Kauravas, she cursed Sri Krishna that just as she had lost her 100 sons, after 36 years he too would lose all his Yadav brethren.

The Passing of Sri Krishna

On one occasion sage Durvasa, son of sage Atri and wife Anasuya, known both for his benevolence and anger, put Sri Krishna and Rukmini to test. He asked them for rice and milk to eat. After he had finished eating, he asked Sri Krishna to smear the leftover rice and milk over his body. Sri Krishna obediently followed Durvasa's instructions. He smeared the rice and the milk all over his body except the soles of the feet. Pleased with Sri Krishna, the sage blessed him that all of his body smeared by the rice and milk would be invulnerable to injury that could cause death.

One day, when Sri Krishna was asleep in the forest, a hunter mistook his feet for the ears of a deer and fired an arrow that hit the sole of Sri Krishna's foot. The hunter later regretted what he had done, but it was too late; the injury was to the only part of the body that was not protected by Durvasa's blessing. Sri Krishna died of the injury, returning to his abode in Vaikunth.

Worship of Sri Krishna

Two of the four major Hindu pilgrimages — Jagannath temple at Puri, and the other at Dwarka, are dedicated to Sri Krishna. Innumerable temples dedicated to him are situated in India and at many places around the world. A temple stands in his place of birth, and the entire region where he spent his childhood is considered sacred. Each year, millions of devotees circumambulate the Govardhan hill.

A magnificent temple devoted to Sri Krishna, known there as **Vithoba** or **Vithala**, and Rukmini is located at Pandharpur in Maharashtra. Hundreds of thousands of devotees visit it every year.

Sri Krishna's birthday and the Holi festival are celebrated with great fervour. Innumerable poems, songs and prayers are recited to seek union with him. He is truly every person's god — simple, straightforward and loving. To be united with him is to be united in eternal bliss.

15

Gautam Buddha

GAUTAM BUDDHA

Gautam Buddha is said to be the ninth incarnation of Vishnu. However, many do not agree. They feel that the theory of his being an incarnation of Vishnu was advanced to create misunderstanding amongst people. We cannot, however, overlook the fact that Gautam Buddha was born in India, where he attained *Nirvana* and went on to influence Hindu religious thought. Despite originating in India, Buddhism did not continue to attract adherents in India as it did in other countries. In 1193, marauders led by Bakhtiyar Khalji sacked the great Buddhist university of Nalanda. Thousands of monks were slaughtered, triggering the decline of Buddhism in India. However, it thrived mightily in South-East Asia. There are almost 350 million Buddhists around the world.

Siddharth was born in a garden in Lumbini to Mahamaya and Shudhodhan, ruler of a small kingdom on the present Indo-Nepal border. Mahamaya was enroute to her father's home when she delivered the baby boy. She passed away a week later, and the upbringing of the son was entrusted to the second queen, Prajapati.

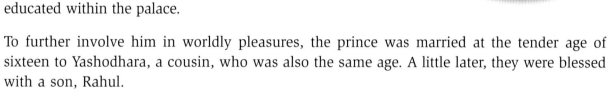

Astrologers predicted that Siddharth would one day either be an emperor or an ascetic who would renounce the pleasures of the world and show humankind the way to eternal bliss. King Shudhodhan desired that he should become an emperor. To ensure that he would not be attracted to asceticism, he decided to completely isolate the child from everyday realities and confined him within the palace in an environment of comfort and luxury. He was also educated within the palace.

To further involve him in worldly pleasures, the prince was married at the tender age of sixteen to Yashodhara, a cousin, who was also the same age. A little later, they were blessed with a son, Rahul.

Renunciation is born out of detachment and aversion to worldly things. The king wanted to keep his son away from this. What is not to be can never be. One day, when the prince wanted to go for a drive, the king arranged that he should visit the best places, and bring back happy memories. Despite strict instructions to the charioteer, the prince managed to persuade him to change the route. For the first time, Siddharth saw a sick man, an old man and a dead person being carried in a funeral procession. Life was never to be the same for him. Shocked at the sufferings in life, he decided to renounce his princely existence and go in search of the Truth.

Despite much dissuasion from his family, at the age of 29, one night he slipped away from home when everyone was fast asleep. He joined two Brahmin hermits. Together they meditated to find the root cause of suffering. In search of the truth, Siddharth visited the wise and the learned. Going from one place to another, he met numerous saints, sages and ascetics but his questions remained unanswered.

With five other friends he then decided on performing hard penance. But even after six years, no success was achieved. The physical hardship was so severe that all the flesh wasted away from his body. He appeared like a living skeleton. Many times he swooned. Then he realized that fasting and penance were of no avail. When a farmer's daughter offered him skimmed milk

he took it. Some say it was milk porridge that she had offered. This offended his friends and they left him.

With some rest, Siddharth felt better. He began meditating alone under a Peepal tree. On the 29th day, as he sat meditating in the evening, he felt the presence of a divine light. Suddenly, he understood the cause of all suffering. He had found the answers to his questions. He was enlightened. From Siddharth Gautam, he was now Gautam Buddha — The Enlightened One.

For a considerable period of time, the Buddha was uncertain whether he should teach what he had experienced and learnt. He felt that with people lost in their own selfish ends, in greed and jealousy, they would not appreciate the path of righteousness, which was difficult to understand and practise. However, in a vision, he was directed to teach what he had personally felt. There are always people who seek the truth. They need a true teacher. So the Buddha became a teacher. At Sarnath, near Varanasi, Buddha delivered his first sermon to the five companions who had earlier accompanied him. Together they formed the first Sangha of Buddhist monks.

Buddha's Teachings

The Buddha proclaimed that there were four eternal truths:
1. There is suffering in life.
2. There are causes for this suffering.
3. This suffering can be avoided.
4. There is a middle path to avoid suffering.

He further explained that to move on the middle path, there were eight essentials:
1. Correct vision: one needed to be able to see the reality.
2. Correct resolve: one's thoughts must be based upon the truth.
3. Correct speech: one's speech must be free of abuse, falsehood, blame, slander and gossip.
4. Correct deeds: one's deeds should not harm or hurt others or one's self.
5. Correct livelihood: one's vocational life must be based upon ethics and morals.
6. Correct exercise: one must maintain physical and emotional health.
7. Correct memories: one's happy memories promote happiness and lead one to divinity.
8. Correct meditation: one must be able to concentrate and look inwards to find peace.

The Buddha explained that he was not a god. He was simply enlightened. He was only teaching what he had experienced. It did not need divine intervention. Anyone could do it by understanding the true nature of the mind, control of thoughts and through meditation. Buddha preached about human suffering and how it could be avoided. He preached the need for love, peace and non-violence.

He explained that everything was impermanent; that the perception of the self was an illusion; that suffering comes from a confused mind. He said nothing was predestined. One action led to another. He further emphasized that only that must be accepted which is in harmony with one's experiences.

The Buddha did not deny existing religious knowledge or speak against the prevalent Hindu way of life. He spoke only of what had been revealed to him. He addressed his followers in the local language, one that they could understand: Pali. He travelled along the north-eastern Gangetic plain preaching his doctrine and the need for discipline. The rich and the poor, the higher castes and the lower castes

formed his audience. As he travelled far and wide, the ranks of his followers swelled. Many Hindus acknowledged him as the ninth incarnation of Vishnu.

Siddharth Gautam

Buddhism was easily accepted in several countries around India probably because it was in harmony with prevalent local religious thought, and the two could co-exist. Since a large proportion of his followers belonged to the Mongolian race, Buddha is often depicted with Mongolian facial features.

However, when describing him to son Rahul, Siddharth's wife explained that he was of Aryan lineage, with a body of a leader amongst the noble warriors. He had a moonlike face with a well-formed nose, blue eyes, dark eyebrows and a determined jaw. Handsome, sensitive and well-mannered, he had a high sense of morality. He walked gracefully. Everyone respected him.

From the description it is evident that Siddharth Gautam was a typical Hindu Kshatriya in looks. He was tall and had a well-built body, like one born of royal blood. He could well have been mistaken for a general.

The Buddha

The personality of the Buddha as represented in the ancient texts describes him as a fit and athletic person, competent in martial arts like any prince. Well educated and interested in a wide range of subjects, he had a deep understanding of religious and philosophical concepts. A good teacher, he could hold sway over his audiences. Calm in the most difficult of situations, he was deft at handling situations with all kinds of people.

Buddhism

Many people adopted Buddhism because of its simplicity. After the Great War of Kalinga, when a large number of soldiers died needlessly, Emperor Ashok also adopted the message of love and non-violence. Many followed suit. Buddhism grew under this brief spell of royal patronage, spreading into eastern and south-eastern Asia. It found easy acceptance along with the existing local religious and cultural beliefs. However, within India, on seeing many Hindus adopting Buddhism, some sections of the clergy felt threatened and deliberately misinterpreted the teachings to hurt Buddhist sentiments. Whereas Buddhism grew in many countries, its growth remained stagnant in India.

The Buddha's Passing Away

The Buddha passed away at the age of eighty. After a meal, he suddenly fell ill. He asked his faithful disciple Ananda to place a bed for him between two trees, and left this world. His last words were: "All composite things pass away. Diligently strive for your own salvation." The body was cremated and the ashes were divided into eight portions to establish eight Stupas around the world.

Worship of the Buddha

There are Buddhist temples not only in India but in many other countries where Buddhism flourishes. Buddhist temples have idols of Buddha. Many have magnificent golden images. The Buddha is mostly depicted sitting cross-legged with his eyes closed in deep meditation. The serenity and peace on his face are noteworthy. At some places, the Buddha is shown standing, or even lying down. The full moon falling in May is designated as Buddha Purnima.

16

The Navgrah

THE NAVGRAH

Hindus accord a position of special importance to the *Navgrah* or the nine planets. At all religious ceremonies, after making the first offering to Sri Ganesh, Hindus make the next offering to the Navgrah.

According to Hindu belief, God resides in all things, places and people. Thus, everyone is connected to all others, through God. We are all children of the same God. Brothers and sisters influence each other in a home. Similarly, as children of God we influence each other. The greatest influence upon everyone is that of the nine planets. They are in constant motion. Their influence varies with their position. They influence the destinies of nations and the life of every individual. An individual's horoscope is cast on the basis of the time and place of birth. A horoscope is said to predict one's destiny, based upon the configuration of the nine planets at the time of birth and changes that occur over the years.

Does this mean that once the destiny of an individual is cast, it cannot be changed? No, that is not so. The position of the planets is only an indication of their influence at a particular time and place. This indication is not a force. It is at best a suggestion. On the contrary, human effort is a definite force. Through positive actions, the influence of the stars can be altered.

In harmony with Hindu belief, each of the nine planets is personified. Each exerts a definite influence, which can be altered through offerings to these planets, to placate them and keep them happy. For this, one must know some basic facts about the nine planets.

Surya — the Sun

The first and foremost of the nine celestial bodies is *Surya*, the Sun.

Surya is the son of the sage Kashyap and wife Aditi. He is also known by the name **Savita**. It is said that once, when the demons attacked the gods and defeated them, a greatly distressed Aditi offered prayers to Surya, who was born as her son. He defeated the demons and established righteousness. As Aditi's son, he is also known as **Aditya**. He is said to have married Sanghya, daughter of Vishvakarma. He is also known to have had sons and daughters by Chhaya, Kunti and Aruni. Shani, Yama, Karna, Sugriva and the Ashvinikumars — Revant and Bhaya — are prominent amongst his sons and daughters.

Surya is depicted with two arms, carrying a lotus in each hand. There is a golden crown on his head, and a gem-studded necklace adorns his neck. He sits on a lotus throne and rides a chariot drawn by seven horses.

According to the **Markandey Purana**, Surya is like Brahma. The world arises from him and resides within him. Like the elements, Surya is eternal. He is like Brahma, Vishnu and Shiva. Like them, he creates, protects and destroys. He is also known as **Surya Narayan**. To please Surya, one must make an offering to him every day. *Surya Namaskar*, or salutation to the sun, is the most popular form of Hindu prayer. Devotees are known to chant 12 mantras facing the morning sun, and offering water to which some red sandalwood, rice, red flowers and kusha are added. To please Surya, devotees also read or listen to **Harivansh Purana**, and wear a ruby ring. Charitable gifts of wheat, jaggery (brown sugar), copper, gold and red fabric are considered auspicious.

The **Atharva-Veda** praises the sun. In 17/1/30, it is said:
The rising sun destroys all kinds of diseases. It protects one from all causes of death.

In the **Atharva-Veda**, 5/30/15, it is said:
To break the bondage of death, stay connected with the light of the sun.

Again, in the **Atharva-Veda**, 8/1/4, it is said:
To live in the light of the sun is like living in the land of immortality.

Astrologers suggest that the sun presides over the head. It is a favourable sign and represents the ego and the self, and also creativity, spontaneity, health and vitality.

Chandrama — the Moon

The second of the nine planets is *Chandrama*, the Moon.

He is the son of the sage Atri and wife Anasuya. He is depicted with two hands, holding a mace in one and blessing devotees with the other. His clothes, chariot and the ten horses that draw it are spotlessly white. There is a golden crown on his head, and a pearl necklace adorns

his neck. Like Surya, Chandrama also sits on a lotus throne.

Chandrama was married to the 27 daughters of Daksh Prajapati. They form the 27 lunar asterisms. Of his 27 wives, he was most fond of Rohini. This offended the others. In protest, they returned to their father's home. The enraged Daksh cursed Chandrama that he would suffer from a debilitating disease. Chandrama sought the help of Shiva, who offered him protection by placing him on his forehead. Since Daksh was insistent that Chandrama be returned, Shiva sought the help of Vishnu. To resolve the dilemma, Vishnu gave Chandrama two forms; one was for Daksh and the other for Shiva. In this way, Daksh got his way, while Chandrama remained a free agent. Yet, because of the aftermath of the curse, Chandrama cyclically wanes for 15 days before regaining his former glory in the next 15 days.

Chandrama is the god of the mind, and helps to keep it under control. The mind is fickle and wavering. It resides in the forehead in between the two eyebrows. When *tilak* is applied there, Chandrama appreciates it. Shiva wears the crescent moon on the forehead. This is symbolic of his being a great yogi. Lovers have always drawn inspiration from the moon. Women offer prayers to Chandrama seeking happiness in their married life and long life for their husbands.

Lack of blessings from Chandrama causes mental and breathing problems. To please him, one must fast on Mondays, pray to Shiva and wear a pearl in a silver ring. One must give rice, camphor, white clothes, silver, conch shell, white sandalwood, white flowers, sugar, curds and pearls in charity. Offering of *kheer* (rice porridge) from a copper vessel to Chandrama on a full moon night pleases him.

Astrologers suggest that the moon is associated with a person's emotional make-up, unconscious habits, rhythms, memories and moods. It is also linked with the mother, maternal instincts, and the domestic arena. It is a melancholic sign.

Mangal — the Planet Mars

The third of the nine planets is *Mangal*, the planet Mars.

He is the son of Vishnu and Bhumi (Mother Earth). When the demon Hiranyaksh in the form of a pig carried Bhumi to Patal Lok, Vishnu as *Varah-avatar* rescued her. Saved from the clutches of the demon, she assumed her real beautiful form and Vishnu fell in love with her. They were blessed with a son, Mangal.

Mangal wears red clothes and a golden crown. Red necklaces adorn his neck. He has four arms. He carries a trident in one of the right hands and a mace in one of the left hands. With the left hand he assures protection, with the right hand he conveys blessings. His vehicle is a ram — a male sheep.

To please Mangal, one needs to fast on Tuesdays and pray to Shiva or Hanuman. One should read the *Hanuman Chalisa*. One must wear coral in a ring. Wheat, copper, gold, red clothes, jaggery, red flowers, saffron and land may be given in charity.

Astrologers suggest that the planet Mars is associated with energy and ambition. It makes one impulsive, confident and aggressive. Mars is ardent, and presides over the genitals. In matching horoscopes for marital compatibility, the influence of Mars receives special consideration.

Budh — the Planet Mercury

The fourth of the nine planets is *Budh*, the planet Mercury.

Budh is the son of Chandrama and Tara, wife of Brihaspati. It is said that once Chandrama abducted Brihaspati's wife Tara, and they had a son. Brahma named him Budh. Later, Brahma compelled Chandrama to return Tara to Brihaspati. In view of his personality and special abilities, Budh was made a planet by Brahma. Impressed by his intellect, Manu arranged for his daughter Ila to marry Budh. They were blessed with a son, Pururava.

Yellow is symbolic of Budh. His body is like bright oleanders. He wears yellow clothes and wears a garland of yellow flowers. He has four arms. He carries a sword in one of the right hands, a mace and a shield in the left hands, and blesses with the other right hand. He wears a golden crown and beautiful jewellery adorns his neck. He rides a lion.

To please Budh, one must fast on the first day of the new moon. One should wear an emerald in a ring. One should give away ivory, green clothes, coral, emeralds, gold, camphor, a weapon, fruits and a variety of foods in charity.

Astrologers suggest that the planet Mercury is associated with a person's mental capacity and thought patterns. It also determines one's reasoning and communication skills. Hindu thought links Budh with *buddhi* (intelligence).

Brihaspati — the Planet Jupiter

The fifth of the nine planets is *Brihaspati*, the planet Jupiter.

He is the son of the sage Angira and his wife Khyati. He had two wives, Shuba and Tara. Brihaspati is the preceptor of the gods. It was his intelligence that enabled the gods to complete the yagya, which the demons wanted to destroy. Brihaspati managed to keep them away with his mantras.

He wears a golden crown and beautiful jewellery. Clad in yellow clothes, he sits on a lotus throne. He has four arms. In the two left hands he carries a shaft and a vessel. In one of the right hands he carries a *Rudraksh rosary*, and blesses with the other.

Brihaspati is a benevolent planet. He blesses his devotees with prosperity and wisdom, and motivates them to follow the path of righteousness. He protects them from dangers. To please him, one must fast on Thursdays and on the first day of the new moon. One should wear a yellow topaz in a ring. One should give yellow clothes, gold, turmeric, ghee, yellow foods, topaz, a horse, book, honey, salt, sugar, land and an umbrella in charity.

Astrologers suggest that Jupiter is temperate and benign. It is associated with growth, expansion and prosperity. It is also related to higher education, spiritual knowledge and a protective role.

Shukra — the Planet Venus

The sixth of the nine planets is *Shukra*, the planet Venus.

Shukra is the son of sage Bhrigu and wife Puloma. They had three daughters — Arja, Devi and Devyani. Devi was married to Varun, the Sea God. As a devotee of Shiva, Shukra performed penance to obtain the *Sanjivini Mantra*. He later taught this mantra to his disciple Kach, son of Brihaspati. With the help of the *Sanjivini Mantra*, Shukra was able to overcome the gods and become the master of everything.

A guru of the demons, he is very fair. He wears a beautiful crown, and beautiful jewellery adorns his neck. He sits on a white lotus throne. He has four arms. He holds a shaft and a vessel in his two left hands and a *Rudraksh rosary* in one of the right hands, while blessing everyone with the other.

When Vishnu incarnated as Vaman, and asked King Bali for three steps of land, Shukra — as guru of the demons — tried to dissuade Bali from granting the boon, and to make the offer unfruitful, Shukra took the form of a cork and plugged the mouth of the vessel containing the ceremonial water. Vaman pre-empted the move and put a straw in the mouth of the vessel for the water to flow through. This straw blinded one of Shukra's eyes.

To appease Shukra, one should wear diamonds and offer prayers to a cow. One should give silver, gold, diamonds, rice, ghee, curds, sugar, white clothes, white sandalwood, a white horse, white cow and land in charity.

Astrologers suggest that Venus is associated with principles of beauty, harmony and balance. It encourages the urge to unite.

Shani — the Planet Saturn

The seventh of the nine planets is *Shani*, the planet Saturn.

Shani is the son of Surya and his wife Chhaya. Since birth, he was a devotee of Sri Krishna. He would spend all his time in praying to Krishna and meditating upon him. However, his marriage to Chitrrath's daughter changed everything. His wife was simple, devoted and outstanding. One night, desiring a son, she came to Shani who was so deeply engrossed in meditation that he failed to respond. She waited for a long time, but could not attract his attention. Losing her temper in frustration, she cursed that anyone he set his eyes on would be destroyed. When Shani got to know of the curse he apologized and requested that the curse be withdrawn. Since the curse could not be withdrawn completely, the intensity was reduced. Repentant at his folly, Shani keeps his head lowered. His influence is malefic.

Shani's complexion is like that of a blue sapphire. He wears gold jewellery and a gold crown. His clothes are blue. He has four arms. He carries a bow and a trident in the two left hands and an arrow in one of the right hands. He blesses with the other. His vehicle is a vulture. His chariot is built of steel. He draws inspiration from Brahma, the creator, and Yama, the God of Death.

To appease Shani, one should chant the *Mahamrituanjaya Mantra*, and offer sesame seeds, black peas, an iron vessel, oil, black clothes, black umbrella, black shoes, a black cow, sapphire and gold in charity.

Astrologers confirm the malefic influence of the planet Saturn — cold, morose and gloomy. It is associated with restrictions, boundaries and limitations.

Rahu and Ketu

The last two of the nine planets are *Rahu* and *Ketu*.

Rahu, son of Kashyap and wife Sinhika, is a demon. When the gods had obtained amrit, the elixir of immortality, by churning the ocean, Rahu assumed the form of a god, entered their stronghold and drank some of it. When Surya and Chandrama discovered him amongst them, they informed Vishnu, who hastily cut off Rahu's head with his Sudarshan chakra. Since some of the elixir had already gone down Rahu's throat, he did not die. The head and the body remained alive. The head is known as Rahu, and the body as Ketu. Brahma transformed the two into planets.

It is believed that to settle scores with Surya and Chandrama, who had reported his intrusion to Vishnu, Rahu and Ketu are sometimes known to

swallow them, thereby causing either a solar or a lunar eclipse. Since the head and the body are separate, however, Surya and Chandrama manage to escape unscathed.

Rahu looks dreadful. He wears gold jewellery, and has a gold crown on his head. He wears black clothes. He has four arms. In the two left hands he carries a trident and a shield. In one of the right hands, he carries a sword. The other is free to bless people. He uses a lion as a vehicle.

To appease Rahu, one must chant the *Mahamrituanjaya Mantra* and wear an amethyst in a ring. One must give mica, iron, copperware, sesame seeds, blue clothes, black peas, seven grains, oil, blanket and a horse in charity.

Ketu has a dusky complexion, wears black clothes and has a gold crown on his head. He has two arms: in his left hand is a mace, and the right is used for blessing. He uses a vulture as his vehicle.

To appease Ketu, one must chant the *Mahamrituanjaya Mantra*. One should also wear cat's eye, which is a precious grey-coloured stone, in a ring. One must give *Vaidurya* (a gem), oil, sesame, a blanket, a weapon, musk and blue flowers in charity.

Astrology aims at studying the effects of the planets in general, particularly their influence on human beings. Each of the nine planets has been studied in great detail. The capability of the astrologer depends upon the study and analysis of the effect of each of the planets upon one another and how it affects an individual. The malefic effects can be diluted through prayers and offerings.

Worship of the Navgrah

All formal worship starts by praying to Sri Ganesh, after which one prays to the Navgrah, invoking their blessings for peace and happiness. Depending upon the current influence of each of the nine planets, one prays to them individually, and also undertakes fasts and charitable activities to appease them.

17

Indra &
Companion God

INDRA AND COMPANION GODS

Indra is the Lord of the *Devas* — the gods who reside in heaven and maintain the elements such as Agni (Fire), Varun (Water), Vayu (Air) and Surya (Sun). There is a constant struggle between the *Devas*, who enforce morality and righteousness, and the *Asuras*, who oppose such enforcement. Whenever the situation goes out of control, the Devas, led by Indra, seek the help of the Hindu Trinity — Brahma, Vishnu and Shiva.

Indra — the Chief of Gods

In Hindu scriptures, Indra is described as the King of Gods. He is also the god of weather and war. Son of Dyaus Pita, a minor deity, Indra is mentioned in the Rig-Veda along with Agni, the Fire God. Some say he is the son of the sage Kashyap and wife Aditi. He is described as the Supreme Deity in early Vedic literature.

Indra is described as a powerful warrior, with four arms and a ruddy complexion. He rides the celestial elephant Airavata. When riding a chariot his speed is said to be like that of thought. His main weapon is the

Vajra (thunderbolt), though sometimes he also carries a bow, arrows, or lances. A great soldier, he is known to have recovered the cows stolen by the Asuras. He is also known to have brought the great mountains under control. He is reputed to have killed the demon Vritra, who had stolen all the water.

Fond of Soma, an alcoholic beverage, he is susceptible to pride and feels insecure whenever someone outdoes him. On one occasion, frustrated because the people of Gokul were not worshipping him, he caused torrential rains to create havoc and teach the people a lesson. To humble his pride, Sri Krishna lifted the Govardhan hill, and the people took shelter under it for several days.

Once intoxicated under the influence of Soma and pride, Indra had an affair with Ahalya, wife of the sage Gautam. The sage cursed him that his reign as king of gods would be disastrous and humiliating, and that he would lose his manhood. This is why Indra is so insecure. Many demon kings repeatedly humiliated him. Ravan's son Meghnad defeated him, and earned the sobriquet 'Indrajit'. Ravan had taken him captive, but released him on Brahma's request. It was not until Sri Ram killed Meghnad and Ravan that Indra's position was redeemed.

On another occasion, Prahlad defeated Indra and took over Swarg Lok. Brihaspati advised him to seek the good qualities of Prahlad. Indra disguised himself as a Brahmin and went to Prahlad, who accepted him as a pupil. Prahlad found him to be a good student and taught him many things. He also granted him a boon. Indra asked that Prahlad give him all his good qualities. This is how Indra regained Swarg Lok.

Indra was married to Indrani, daughter of Puloman. He had several sons. Surya, Vali and Arjun (by Kunti) are the better known ones. His son Jayant lost one of his eyes as punishment, when he took the form of a crow and pecked Sita's foot. Sri Ram would have killed him, but when he apologized (on Narad's advice), Sri Ram let him off with a milder punishment.

Indra was worshipped in the early Vedic period, but in present times, he does not enjoy as much prominence.

Agni — the God of Fire

Second only to Indra, Agni is immortal. In Sanskrit, *Agni* literally means *fire*. As a messenger between the gods and the common man, Agni is a medium of sacrifices, which is re-lit every

day and, therefore, is also symbolic of youth. The first word in the **Rig-Veda** is Agni, described as a priest, a divine route to sacrifice and giver of blessings.

In some Hindu scriptures, Agni is described as the son of the sage Kashyap and wife Aditi. In others he is said to be Indra's twin brother, and son of Dyaus Pita and Prithvi. The two sticks that produce fire when rubbed together are also described as Agni's parents. Some say he is the son of Brahma. He was married to Svaha. Kartikeya is said to be his son, either through Svaha, Ganga or the five maidens who received the five sparks sent by Shiva.

Agni is said to be two-faced and red in colour. The two faces are symbolic of the beneficial and destructive attributes of fire. Agni is described as having black eyes and hair, three legs and seven arms. His vehicle is a ram, though goats pull his chariot. Seven beams of light are seen coming out of his body. He is therefore also known as **Sapta Jivh**, meaning *one with seven tongues*. Agni is seen in three forms — fire, lightning and the sun. Agni is also said to be the power of digestion in each individual.

It is explained in the **Ramayan** that just before Sri Ram was ready to proceed to fulfil the purpose for which he had incarnated, and Ravan was to abduct Sita in his absence, unknown even to Lakshman, he handed over Sita to Agni for protection. In exchange, Agni produced a clone of Sita, who went to Lanka with Ravan. After Ravan was killed, and Sita returned, she was asked to undergo the Agni Pariksha (the test of fire) to prove that she was pure. Lakshman, Hanuman, Sugriva and all others present were shocked. Sita insisted that a pyre be set up. As people watched in horror and shock, Sita's clone entered the fire and unknown to anyone the real Sita walked out.

Agni is always considered to be the great purifier. All Hindu scriptures highly commend yagyas where mantras are chanted and sacrifices offered. To this day, *havan* is conducted daily in many Hindu homes. In others, it is conducted on special occasions. Each mantra chanted always begins with *Aum* and ends with *Svaha* — the name of Agni's wife. This symbolizes that she is a witness when sacrifices are offered to her husband Agni.

Amongst Hindus, a marriage is not complete until the couple takes marital vows before a fire. Going around the fire seven times is a mandatory part of a Hindu wedding ceremony. When someone dies, Hindus consign the body to fire, considering it the most purifying of all agents. Agni continues to be worshipped with both awe and respect.

Vayu — the God of Wind

Vayu is the god of air and wind. He is also known as **Vata** and **Pavan**. *Vata,* similar to the word *vita* in Latin, or *vital* in English, refers to *life*. It is not possible to live without air. Once breathing stops, life ends. Vayu, therefore, is one of the five elements necessary for life, and accepted as the *Panchmahabhuta* by Hindus.

Vayu and Anjana had a son, Hanuman. As a child, Hanuman once felt hungry and mistook the sun for a fruit. He leaped up into the sky to eat it. Seeing him rushing towards the sun, the alarmed Indra hurled his Vajra at him. Hanuman fell down to the ground and hurt his jaw. Seeing this, Vayu was angry and carried him away to Patal Lok. With Vayu gone, everyone felt suffocated. The gods realised their blunder and hurried to Vayu, pleading for mercy. To please him, they blessed Hanuman. Brahma and Indra granted many boons. Thus was Hanuman blessed that no weapon could slay him, and that he could only die if he so willed it.

On one occasion, Kunti, the wife of Pandu, invoked Vayu and had a son Bhim by him. As one of the five Pandavas, Bhim plays a crucial role in the Mahabharat. Both Bhim and Hanuman are addressed with the epithet *Vayuputra* (son of Vayu).

Vayu had several wives, and had many children through them. On one occasion, he was enamoured by the beauty of King Kushnabh's hundred daughters, and asked them to marry him. They refused, saying that they would not marry without their father's permission. Vayu lost his temper at their refusal and cursed them, so that their limbs became crooked. The king then persuaded Brahmadati to marry them. On his touch, they became normal once again.

Vayu is said to have revealed the **Vayu Purana**, one of the eighteen principal Puranas. Divided into four sections, the Vayu Purana explains the laws of duty and glorifies Shiva. Beginning with the creation of elements, the Purana goes on to describe the various eras and evolution of the incarnations, praising Shiva.

Five deities known as **Prana**, **Apana**, **Vyana**, **Udana** and **Samana** symbolize Vayu. These control the vital breath, wind, touch, digestion and excretion. Different deities are said to control the many functions in the body. In the **Brhadaranyaka Upanishad**, it is said that once the gods who control the functions of the body got into an argument as to who amongst them was most important. One by one, they withdrew their support. Vision was lost, but still one lived. The limbs failed, but life continued. However, when Vayu withdrew his support, the support of all other gods failed. It was then that they realised that unless Vayu lent his support, life was not possible. As the vital breath, Vayu is the god of life, and bound to be an object of worship.

Varun — the God of Oceans

Varun is the god of oceans, and rivers that give their water to the oceans. Varun also looks after the souls of those who die by drowning. He is therefore also a god of the dead. He is said to be omniscient and omnipotent. He can bless one with immortality.

In the **Rig-Veda**, Varun is mentioned with Indra as **Indravaruna**. As Indra became the king of gods, Varun was associated with rain and water. He is also mentioned with Mitra

as **Mitravaruna**. Both are mentioned as Adityas. Religious texts describe him as the son of the sage Kashyap and his wife Aditi. Brahma declared him the king of the waters. Varun is depicted in white, wearing gold armour and holding a noose made of a snake.

Varun had several wives, and many children by them. Once enamoured by Bhadra, wife of the sage Utathya, Varun abducted her and hid her under the sea. The sage was angry to find his wife missing. Narad told him what had happened. Infuriated, the sage drank the entire ocean to make it dry. Varun was compelled to return Bhadra. The sage forgave him when he apologized.

The sage Agastya is said to be Varun's son through Urvashi. Sri Ram, Sita and Lakshman visited sage Agastya when they were in exile. The sage is said to have presented celestial weapons to Sri Ram. The sage went to Ayodhya to congratulate Sri Ram when he became king.

At Agni's, request Varun presented Arjun a chariot with horses, the Gandiv bow and two inexhaustible quivers. He is also said to have presented Sri Krishna with the mace known as Kaumodki and the Sudarshan Chakra. When Brahma asked the gods to help Sri Ram in his war against Ravan, Varun sent his son Sushen in the form of a monkey.

When Sri Ram and his forces reached the sea that separated them from Lanka, they wondered how to cross it. Vibhishan said nothing could stop the Master of the Universe, and that the God of the Ocean would make way for him. Lakshman, impatient as ever, suggested that Sri Ram dry up the ocean to enable the forces to go on. But Sri Ram saw wisdom in Vibhishan's suggestion, and sat down in prayer to the God of the Ocean.

Three days of prayer went by, but there was no response. Sri Ram thought Lakshman was right in suggesting firm action. Even in friendship, one sometimes needs to use fear. He said, "Lakshman, bring my bow and arrows. I will dry the ocean. It is not proper to implore a stupid person, just as friendship with a rogue is not worthwhile." Lakshman was delighted as Sri Ram raised his bow to set the ocean on fire. The fish and serpents were distressed.

Then Varun appeared before Sri Ram. He held Sri Ram's feet and said, "Forgive me my faults, O Lord! Ether, air, fire, water and earth are dull and slow. It is through your *Maya* that they sustain life. Each has a definite responsibility. Each works within certain limitations. I can understand why you have inspired fear in me. By your command, the ocean will dry up. This will only bring me discredit. Please tell me what you desire."

Sri Ram was pleased to hear Varun. He said, "Dear friend, could you suggest an alternative method so that the monkey troops can safely cross the ocean?" Varun responded, "My Lord, the brothers Nala and Nila are endowed with the ability to build a bridge over the ocean. I shall also help them as much as I can. Let the arrow that you have shot, rid the northern coast of the criminals that inhabit it." The idea of building a bridge appealed to Sri Ram. Varun bowed before Sri Ram and took his leave.

Just as one cannot do without air, one also cannot do without water. A *kalash* containing water is an important part of every formal Hindu religious ceremony. It is a symbol of auspiciousness. Water is also sprinkled and consumed at the beginning of each prayer. This is a way of silently worshipping Varun.

Kama — the God of Love

Kama, the God of Love, occupies an important place as a companion god with Indra. Every time Indra has felt threatened with the sacrifice and penance of a saint or a sage, he has sought the help of Kama, and beautiful maidens to distract seekers away from spiritual growth, with the lure of earthly pleasures. Many a saint has succumbed to the wiles of Kama.

Kama is the son of Prajapati Dharm by his wife Shraddha. He is described as a handsome man holding a bow made of sugarcane and arrows made of flowers. He is married to Rati. Together, they are known as the gods of love. Kama has a close friend in Vasant, who is the lord of the spring season. Kama's vehicle is a parrot.

On one occasion, the sage Narad decided to live in a hermitage in the Himalayas. The river Ganga flowed close by. The atmosphere was calm and peaceful. Focussing his mind on the feet of his Lord, he offered prayers and austerities. Narad's devotion to the Lord made Indra anxious. Would Narad usurp his position through powers gained from the Lord? To prevent this from happening, Indra sought the help of Kama.

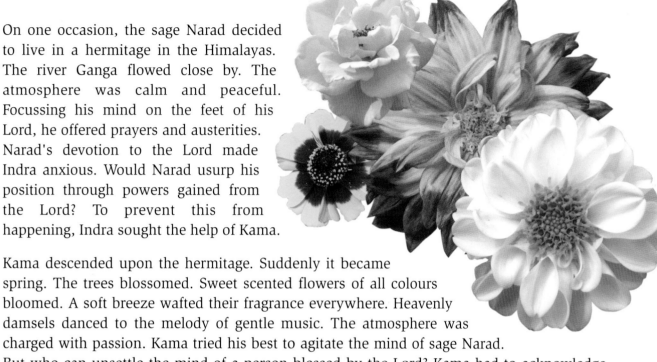

Kama descended upon the hermitage. Suddenly it became spring. The trees blossomed. Sweet scented flowers of all colours bloomed. A soft breeze wafted their fragrance everywhere. Heavenly damsels danced to the melody of gentle music. The atmosphere was charged with passion. Kama tried his best to agitate the mind of sage Narad. But who can unsettle the mind of a person blessed by the Lord? Kama had to acknowledge defeat, and feared the worst from Narad. To atone for his folly, Kama held the sage's feet and sought forgiveness. Narad was not angry, and let Kama go without admonishing him. However, his victory over Kama gave rise to pride, which was the cause of his humiliation when he wanted to marry Mohini.

Hindus appreciate that *dharma*, *arth*, *kama* and *moksha* are the four basic aims of life, and are driving forces that keep mankind on the move. Since *kama* pertains to sensual pleasures, it is important to keep it under control.

At one time a demon, Taraka, was creating havoc all over the world. The gods tried to control him, but without any success. He was invincible. When nothing worked, the gods went to Brahma, who told them that only a son of Lord Shiva could kill the demon. Sati was reborn as Parvati. She had undergone great austerities and penance. Shiva had renounced everything and sat in meditation. It was best to send Kama to upset the serenity of Shiva's mind. He could then be convinced to marry Parvati.

When the gods expressed their plan to Kama, he was doubtful about its success. He knew that if it failed, this would mean death for him at the hands of Shiva. But motivated by the good of all, he agreed to risk his life. Armed with his five arrows, Kama brought the whole world under the sway of his powers.

All reasoning was forgotten. Lust overtook all creatures. Self-restraint, spiritual wisdom, religious vows, morality, yoga and even prayers fell an easy prey to the strange force that enveloped everything. The whole world was agitated with passion. This lasted until Kama reached where Shiva sat in meditation.

The sight of Shiva terrified Kama, but he could not retreat. Summoning his powers, he ushered in spring. Flowers appeared everywhere. Nature overflowed with love. Bees hummed and birds sang. A cool breeze fanned the flames of passion. But Shiva sat unmoved. Frustrated at his failure, Kama climbed up a mango tree, and shot his five arrows at Shiva. They hit him in the chest. Shiva came out of the trance. When he saw Kama hidden in the mango tree, he opened his third eye. Kama was reduced to ashes. The gods looked on in shock.

Kama's wife, Rati, fainted when she heard of her husband's fate. She rushed to Shiva to seek mercy. Moved by the pleading of the helpless woman, Shiva said that Kama would now exist in a bodiless form. He would be born again as Pradyumna, a son of Sri Krishna, and his influence over everyone would continue. Satisfied with Shiva's response, Rati went away.

Kama continues to influence everyone's life. Appreciating the need for fulfilment, the sage Vatsyayan wrote the **Kama Sutra**, the first sex manual. Even after hundreds of years, it continues to provide knowledge on sexual fulfilment. Those who live a balanced life find happiness. Whoever gives in to lust, follows the path of disaster.

Kuber — the God of Wealth

Kuber is the God of Wealth. He is also known as **Dhanpati**. Son of the sage Vishrava and his wife Devarnini, he is also known as **Vaishravan**. In response to his sacrifices

and penance offered to Brahma, he was granted several boons. Kuber sought that he should become immortal; that he should be accepted as a god, with charge of all wealth. He also wished to be the guardian of the northern sector. Brahma, besides granting these boons, asked Vishvakarma to make the Pushpak *viman* as a vehicle for him.

Satisfied that Brahma had granted all that he desired, Kuber settled in Lanka with the *Yakshas* and the *Gandharvas* to enjoy a life of pleasure. Meanwhile, his half brothers Ravan and Kumbhkaran had also obtained boons that gave them the power to rule the three worlds. With their new-found power, they threw Kuber out of Lanka. They also took over the Pushpak *viman*. Kuber moved his residence to Mount Kailash and built his capital Alka. Kuber was married to Bhadra. They had two sons, Nalkuber and Manigriv.

With his great wealth, Kuber was given to pride. On one occasion, to show off his wealth he invited Shiva to have a meal with him in his capital city. Shiva could sense his pride and refused saying that he was preoccupied. Since he did not want to disappoint Kuber, he would send Sri Ganesh to represent him. Kuber laughed that Sri Ganesh was only a child. Yet out of courtesy, he could not turn down Shiva's suggestion.

Sri Ganesh was well received on his arrival. Kuber had doubts if Sri Ganesh would appreciate all that he had to offer, but still laid out a great feast that included a large variety of dishes. In no time, Sri Ganesh ate everything. He desired more. All the cooked food was eaten. Fruits that could be eaten without cooking were offered while more fresh food was prepared. But Sri Ganesh's appetite was insatiable. Finally, even the raw ingredients were exhausted. Sri Ganesh still asked for more. Annoyed that food had stopped coming, Sri Ganesh mocked Kuber.

Afraid of the wrath of Sri Ganesh, Kuber rushed to Shiva. He apologized for having secretly desired to show off his wealth and prosperity to Shiva and Sri Ganesh. Shiva offered a few stems of durva grass to Sri Ganesh and his appetite was satiated. Only then did Sri Ganesh calm down.

Vishvakarma — the Engineer God

Vishvakarma is the engineer amongst gods. The name Vishvakarma is formed of two words. *Vishva* means *the world* or *universe*, and *karma* means *deed* or *action*. Taken together, the words mean *the universal builder*.

Since a lot of machinery and equipment is used in factories and even homes, it is customary to seek the blessings of Vishvakarma before beginning any work that involves machinery and equipment. This helps prevent accidents and untoward incidents.

Son of Vasu Prabhas and wife Varastri, Vishvakarma was married to a celestial nymph Ghritachi. They had three daughters and several sons. Two of the daughters were married to King Priyavrat, and the third, Sanghya was married to Surya. Since Sanghya could not bear the heat of Surya, on her complaint Vishvakarma cut off one-eighth of Surya's radiance.

With the energy taken away from Surya, Vishvakarma built the Pushpak *viman* (flying machine), the Sudarshan Chakra, a trident for Shiva, and the weapon 'Shakti' for Kartikeya. In the same way, he built innumerable weapons, beautiful ornaments and other useful things for the gods. He built a beautiful palace for Kuber at Lanka, and for Indra, he made the thunderbolt. He is also known to have built a special steel chariot for Shiva when he needed to fight Tripur. The other gods acknowledged him as their engineer.

Vishvakarma's son Nala helped Ram build the bridge across the ocean at Rameshwaram. His other sons specialized in the fields of carpentry, masonry, artistic etching, metals, minerals and other engineering fields. To this day, their successors continue in these fields, many of whom still use the surname Vishvakarma. Vishvakarma was a great craftsman. Through his association with the gods, he too came to be acknowledged as a god.

It is customary to offer prayers to Vishvakarma on the day after Diwali. Many do so on Vishvakarma's birth anniversary. The toolroom or factory machinery and equipment is cleaned, the tools are put together at the place of prayer and formal group prayers organized to appease Vishvakarma. Those who work with machinery every day seek his blessings as a part of the morning prayers.

Yama — the God of Death

Yama is the God of Death, and he lives in Yam Lok. Departed souls live with him. Yam Lok is also known as Yampuri. Two very ferocious four-eyed dogs guard it. As the master of Yam Lok, Yama is also known as Yamraj. It is the law of nature that whosoever is born must die, yet everyone is afraid of death and therefore of Yamraj. When a person has lived the designated life, Yamraj takes away the soul leaving behind the body.

Yama is the son of Surya and Sanghya. His weapon is the mace. In his hand he has *kalsutra* or *kalpash*, a noose that he uses to extract the soul from a person. He uses a male buffalo as a vehicle. Amongst his messengers of death are the pigeon, the owl and the crow. Seated on his throne of judgement he summons every individual one by one. Chitragupta presents the account of their good and bad deeds. Yamraj passes judgement on the basis of this account. He is the final judge of an individual's good and bad deeds.

Yama has several wives. Of them Sushila, Vijaya and Hemamala are best known. Of his many sons, Yudhishthir is the best known. Both Yama and Yudhishthir are extremely fair in their judgement of right and wrong. They are, therefore, also known as Dharmraj — king of justice. The river Yamuna is known to be Yama's twin sister. Prayers are offered to both of them on the day Raksha Bandhan is celebrated.

Yama is known for his righteousness and justice. It is mentioned in the Puranas that on one occasion, the sage Mandavya was enraged at Yama and cursed him that he would be born as a human being. It was for this reason that Yama was born through a maid as Dhritrashtra.

To enable individuals to get rid of their past sins, Yama established pilgrimages through Yameshwar and Yamaditya temples, where one could attain one's desires through sacrifices and penance. The 14th day of the lunar month that is a Tuesday is considered most auspicious to go on this pilgrimage. It is believed that bathing and offering prayers in these temples spares one of the punishments in hell. One is also spared from going to Yam Lok.

It is also believed that after pilgrimage to these temples, when one offers *shraddh* to the forefathers, and offers prayers to Yameshwar and Yamaditya, one is free from the bond of debt to the forefathers. Many people offer a lighted *deepak* or earthenware oil lamp to Yama a day before Diwali, and also on other occasions to gain his blessings.

The religious scriptures give accounts of the sage Markandey escaping the wrath of Yama even when Shiva had personally granted him only sixteen years of life. It was possible only through Markandey's devotion to Shiva, who turned away Yama to protect his devotee. On another occasion, Yama had to return Satyavan to his wife Savitri, who persisted in following Yama with devotion and respect. He granted Savitri several boons for her devotion, but would not return her husband. Finally, she trapped him by asking for a hundred sons. This was not possible without Satyavan, and Yama had to give in.

Other Gods and Demi-gods

There are several other gods like **Surya**, **Chandrama**, **Budh** and **Brihaspati** who are companions to Indra, the king of gods. These gods are a part of the *Navgrah*, and have already been discussed. Brihaspati is especially respected as the guru amongst gods. **Kartikeya**, son of Shiva, is revered as the commander of the army of the gods. **Dhanvantri**, who emerged at the time of Samudramanthan holding the vessel of amrit, is said to be the physician amongst gods.

Yaksh is a class of demi-gods who attend upon Kuber, the God of Wealth. They are the offspring of the sage Pulastya. **Gandharvas** are a class of celestial beings who are said to be the singers and musicians to the gods. **Apsaras** are a class of celestial nymphs that reside in Swarg Lok. They are exceptionally beautiful and have the ability to change forms. They are dancers and musicians. As we have read, Indra is known to have sent them many times to distract sages and others from their spiritual endeavours.

18

The Eternal Ganga

THE ETERNAL GANGA

Hindus have always revered nature. Most temples and places of pilgrimage are situated deep in the hills or mountains, or alongside rivers, lakes or near the sea. Hindus pray to the sun, the moon and the other planets. They believe that the Navgrah hold sway over the destinies of nations, communities and individuals.

Rain may just be a natural phenomenon to most people. To Hindus, good or scanty rainfall, floods and drought, storms and hurricanes are the work of Indra, who controls these to their benefit or detriment. To the modern scientist, the sun is just a source of light, heat or energy. But to Hindus the sun is a god — Surya. The moon too is a god — Chandrama. The other planets, too, are personified — Mars as Mangal, Jupiter as Brihaspati or Saturn as Shani.

Just like the planets, the hills, mountains and rivers are all personified. One senses the invisible hands of different gods that support these. The rivers are goddesses giving magnanimously like a mother. When angry, they punish the children harshly. Of all the rivers, Hindus hold Ganga as most sacred. It has not only showered prosperity through its long journey from the Himalayas to the sea, but has been a source of spiritual growth.

The Holy River

Brahma created Ganga from the water he had collected by washing Vishnu's feet. When Ganga came from heaven to earth, Shiva received her in his hair. Having come in contact with all the members of the Hindu Trinity, Ganga is undoubtedly the holiest of all rivers.

Emerging from the serene atmosphere of Gaumukh, deep in the Himalayas and flowing over 2500 kilometres to join the Bay of Bengal, the bountiful Ganga is revered by Hindus throughout its journey. It is a source of great prosperity and happiness to millions of farmers. On its banks are situated great centres of learning and pilgrimage that have always been dear to the gods and mankind. The water of the Ganga has magical properties; for one, bacteria fail to thrive in it, so bottled Ganges water rarely goes stale.

Some believe that Ganga is the daughter of the King of the Himalayas, Himavant and his wife Mena. This would mean that Parvati and Ganga are sisters. The goddess Ganga is always depicted as a very beautiful lady wearing white garments that are pink-tinged. She holds a water pot in one hand and a white lotus in the other. She stands on a *makar*, which is a crocodile with a tail of a fish, in a Himalayan lake. There are many stories about her emergence in this world. The most popular one concerns King Bhagirath.

There was once a king named Sagar, who was conducting his 100th Ashvamedh Yagya. Threatened by the great power that King Sagar would have after the sacrifice was completed, Indra stole the horse and released him near a place where a sage, Kapil, was in deep meditation and penance. The king had sixty thousand sons. He sent them to look for the horse of the Ashvamedh sacrifice. When the sons found the horse grazing near the place where the sage was in meditation, they thought he had stolen it and challenged him. Enraged at being disturbed, the sage reduced the sons to ashes with his wrath.

Their successors were told that the sons of Sagar could get salvation only if Ganga flowed over their ashes. Ganga was in heaven, and they were unable to bring her to earth. Later, King Bhagirath, one of the successors went into penance, living in the forests in great discomfort. When Brahma was convinced of Bhagirath's penance, he appeared and granted him a boon.

"Lord! I have all that I need," King Bhagirath said humbly. "All that I now desire is that Ganga should come on earth, granting salvation to the sixty thousand sons of King Sagar."

"So be it," Brahma said. "I am willing to grant your wish. I have Ganga in my kamandal. However, when I release her and she hits the earth, the land would be flooded. Houses would be destroyed. Many people will lose their lives."

King Bhagirath was disappointed to hear this. He thought he had achieved his goal, and yet it continued to elude him. He requested Brahma to suggest a possible solution. He was told that Shiva could help him.

King Bhagirath again went into penance, this time to seek this favour from Shiva. Eventually, Shiva appeared before Bhagirath and told him that he was willing to help him. He would hold Ganga in the tresses on his head before letting it fall to the earth. That way, the shock of the fall would be absorbed and there would be no loss on earth.

When Brahma released Ganga from his kamandal, she thought that by the force of her fall on Shiva's head, he would be pushed into Patal Lok. When Shiva came to know of Ganga's pride, he was enraged. To humble Ganga, Shiva hid her in his tresses, and none could see her.

King Bhagirath was disappointed once again. He sought the help of Shiva and persuaded him to release Ganga from his tresses. When Shiva let loose Ganga, three streams went eastwards and another three westwards. The main stream followed King Bhagirath who rode in his chariot from the Himalayas to the Bay of Bengal. Thus Ganga was able to grant salvation to the sons of Sagar, and to millions of others who followed.

At one point, Ganga entered the sage Jahnu's hermitage and flooded it. Infuriated at this, the sage drank all the water of the Ganga, drying it up. This upset the gods and they persuaded

Jahnu to let Ganga go about her mission. The sage released the water through his ears. Ganga is therefore also known as **Jahnvi**, meaning daughter of the sage Jahnu.

In **Mahabharat**, Vanparv, 85/89-90-93, it is said:
Just as fire burns the fuel, in the same way if one were to bathe in the Ganga even after hundreds of forbidden deeds, the water of the Ganga would cleanse them all. In Satyayug, all pilgrimages produced results. In Tretayug Pushkar, in Dwaparyug Kurukshetra and in Kaliyug Ganga would be most important. The very name of Ganga purifies a sinner. The sight of it is auspicious. Bathing in it or drinking a few drops of her waters purifies seven generations.

In the **Bhagavad Gita**, Sri Krishna says:
Amongst rivers, I am the Ganga.

In the **Padma Purana** it is said that Ganga can wash away the sins of several births. It makes one virtuous, and enables one to find a place in heaven.

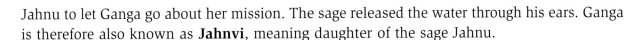

In the **Agni Purana** it is said that Ganga blesses one with *moksha*. Bathing in it is purifying. Those who chant the glory of Ganga gain many virtues. No pilgrimage to a river is holier than the one made to the banks of the Ganga.

In the **Mahabharat**, there is the story of Shantanu who fell in love with Ganga. The episode actually began much earlier, when the eight Vasus once visited the sage Vasishtha. The wife of the Vasu Ah, took a liking to Nandini, a cow belonging to Vasishtha, and asked her husband to get it for her friend Jitvati. Knowing that Vasishtha would not part with it willingly, Ah stole it when Vasishtha was away. On his return Vasishtha learnt through his spiritual powers what had happened. He cursed that the Vasus would be born as human beings. Shocked at what had happened the Vasus rushed to Vasishtha, returned the cow and apologized. The curse could not be withdrawn. He modified it that their life as human beings would be very short, but Ah, who had actually stolen the cow would live a complete lifetime as a human being.

The Vasus went to Ganga to seek her help. They desired that they be born as her sons. When Shantanu approached Ganga she said that she would keep returning to him as long as he did not question her about what she did. He agreed. When they had the first son, Ganga let him drown in the river. Shantanu did not say a word. The same thing happened when the second son was born. When the third and fourth sons were born, they met with the same fate. This went on until seven of their sons had been drowned in the river. When the eighth was to be born, Shantanu could bear it no longer, and took away the son. He was named Dev Vrat, who later became the famed Bhishma Pitamah. But after Shantanu's breaking of his promise, Ganga never returned to him.

Since Ganga carried the five sparks released by Shiva to the Gandharva maidens, Ganga is also said to be the foster mother of **Kartikeya**.

To this day, Ganga continues to be the most worshipped river in the world. Millions of people bathe in it every year. Many important places of pilgrimage and spiritual learning lie along its banks. The Maha Kumbh Melas at Allahabad and Hardwar attract millions of devotees from all over the world every twelve years. Both of these melas are the largest of their kind in the world. Water from the river is part of the prayer paraphernalia in many Hindu homes.

Many Hindus pray that they should die near the Ganga, and their last rites be performed on its banks. Even when that is not possible, the relatives carry the ashes of the dead to be immersed in the Ganga. As in the story of the sons of King Sagar, they searched for moksha, or release from the eternal cycle of births and deaths.

As in the case of the river Ganga, people continue to seek and worship the divinity in the many rivers, mountains and lakes that abound in this ancient land.

19

Divinity
In Animals

DIVINITY IN ANIMALS

Hindu religious scriptures make it evident that just as divinity pervades every pore of a human being, it is equally so in the case of animals. There is a purpose in God having created animals. To accept this purpose is to revere animals.

Animals have been responsible for much of mankind's progress, both physically as well as emotionally. One cannot think of life without the milk from cows and other animals. The male of the species have always helped man to till and irrigate the land, grow food and haul the produce to market. Many animals have helped man travel, just as they have helped the gods. Elephants, horses, mules, camels, yak, reindeer and even the simple donkey have eased mankind's burden. Sheep give us wool, the silkworm provides silk thread, and bees give us honey. Even the pig provides bristles, which find many uses. Living in harmony with animals is an essential part of the Hindu way of life.

Only the later incarnations of Vishnu were in human form. Earlier, he incarnated as a fish, a tortoise, a boar and also as half-man, half-lion. When such incarnations can be divine, the forms of other animals cannot be excluded. They have found equal favour with the gods.

Kuber was the only god to have Vishvakarma's artefact, the Pushpak *viman* as a vehicle. All other gods used animals as vehicles. These have been objects of worship along with their masters.

In the **Shiva Purana** it is mentioned that Sri Ganesh used a mouse as a vehicle. A mouse is self-willed, unrestrained and uncontrollable. These qualities are symbolic of the mind. Such a situation warns one of instability. If one can control the mind just as Sri Ganesh controls the mouse, a devotee can concentrate and achieve much in life. With knowledge of the inner soul, one can control the instability of the mind. It is the mind that binds a person, or takes one towards salvation.

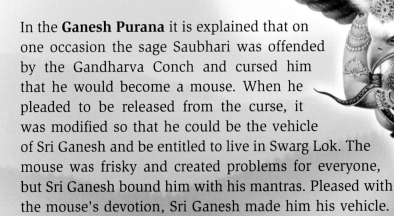

In the **Ganesh Purana** it is explained that on one occasion the sage Saubhari was offended by the Gandharva Conch and cursed him that he would become a mouse. When he pleaded to be released from the curse, it was modified so that he could be the vehicle of Sri Ganesh and be entitled to live in Swarg Lok. The mouse was frisky and created problems for everyone, but Sri Ganesh bound him with his mantras. Pleased with the mouse's devotion, Sri Ganesh made him his vehicle.

Both Brahma and Saraswati have a swan as a vehicle. The swan is revered amongst birds, being known for its ability to separate milk from water. This is symbolic of discernment. It is also known to pick up pearls from the water, another symbolic reference to good judgement. With such qualities, one can find one's way to God.

Vishnu is shown relaxing on the coils of the great Sheshnag, the lord of Patal Lok, with the thousand-headed hood serving as a parasol. Hindus believe that Sheshnag carries the earth on his hood.

Vishnu's vehicle, Garuda, is the king of birds. It is well known for its farsightedness. Equipped with divine powers, it is capable of flying long distances. Garuda is symbolic of the Vedas. It has the great capacity of rejuvenation. When Lakshmi is with Vishnu, they travel together on Garuda. On one occasion, when Narad summoned Garuda to help Sri Ram and Lakshman, who were held captive by a coil of serpents, pride overtook him and Garuda became doubtful if his master was as powerful as he thought him to be. To dispel his doubts Garuda went to Shiva, who guided him to Kakabhusundi, a crow, who was fortunate to have experienced the direct vision of the Supreme Being.

In his incarnation as Sri Ram, Vishnu acknowledges the support of the monkey king Sugriva and his monkey forces. He is also grateful to Jambavan and the bears, to the vulture Jatayu and his brother Sampati.

In the **Bhagavad Gita**, 10, 20, Sri Krishna says:
"Arjun, I am the universal Self that resides in all beings; I am the beginning, the middle and the end of all beings."

In later stanzas, Sri Krishna goes on to say:

"Amongst the horses, I am the celestial horse, Uchaisrava, who emerged during Samudramanthan."

"Amongst the elephants, I am Airavata."
"Amongst the serpents, I am Vasuki."
"Amongst the Nagas, I am Ananta."
"Amongst fish, I am the Shark."
"Amongst cows, I am the celestial cow Kamadhenu."

In the **Devi Bhagwat** it is said that when alone, Lakshmi uses an owl as a vehicle. An owl is day-blind. It can see only at night. When Lakshmi is remembered individually without her consort Vishnu, she travels at night on her vehicle. Since Lakshmi travels alone at night, those who are obsessed with wealth and prosperity operate in darkness. They are unaware of the light of the Sun, which is symbolic of self-knowledge or self-realisation.

Shiva and Parvati use the bull, Nandi, who perceives religious knowledge well. His white colour is symbolic of his capabilities. His four legs are symbolic of the four pillars of religion — compassion, charity, austerity and purity. Through these four qualities, one can attain salvation. Shiva has snakes entwined around his neck and the arms.

Durga uses a lion as a vehicle. The lion is a ferocious, fearless animal, symbolic of strength and virility. The devotees of Durga gradually develop the qualities of a lion. They develop strength through devotion, but often get intoxicated with it. They are capable of defeating their foes.

The other gods also use different animals as vehicles. Indra moves on an elephant, Airavata. Kartikeya uses a peacock as his vehicle. Surya rides a chariot pulled by seven white horses. Mangal rides a male sheep. Budh and Rahu ride a lion. Brihaspati rides a golden chariot pulled by eight horses. Both Shani and Ketu use vultures as their vehicle and create problems for people. The vulture happens to be a bird that is forever on the lookout for carcasses.

Yama, the God of Death, uses a male buffalo as a vehicle. It looks terrible. With its black colour and ferocious looks, it is often equated with an evil spirit and considered inauspicious to look at.

The love for their masters makes animals resemble human friends, in many ways. Sages and saints could live safely in deep forests because of the company of animals like cows, goats, horses, sheep, deer and even smaller animals like dogs, cats and squirrels. Even the birds provide love and care for the little they eat.

Many animals are worshipped with the gods that are served by them. Even in modern times, the cow is known not only for the milk that it provides, but is acknowledged as a 'mother'. During Govardhan pooja, a day after Diwali, cows and bullocks are especially worshipped. Snakes are worshipped during Nag Panchmi. In temple architecture, animals feature almost as much as the gods.

In the **Mahabharat,** it is said that after the Pandavas died one after the other, only Yudhishthir was left behind. He had only a dog as companion. The dog would follow him everywhere. Finally, when Yudhishthir went to Swarg Lok, the dog followed him there also. Yudhishthir was stopped at the gate. Dogs were not permitted to enter Swarg Lok. The dog had been devoted to Yudhishthir, and he did not want to abandon him now. Yudhishthir said, "If my dog cannot accompany me here, I refuse to enter Swarg Lok. You can send me wherever we can go together." Both were admitted to Swarg Lok.

20

Divinity
In Plants

DIVINITY IN PLANTS

Hindus have always revered trees, shrubs and plants. They are a source of food and sustenance. They not only provide medicinal herbs, but are accepted as the foundation of life. The Puranas and other religious texts have accorded great importance to plant life. They have been equated with gods. It is often suggested that they should be accepted as members of the family.

The credibility of the religious texts has been strengthened with scientists having confirmed that plants are living beings. This has also strengthened the belief of the effect of good and bad deeds on rebirth. The devotion and special status granted to some plants is now easier to understand.

According to the religious texts, when people plant trees and care for them, the plants are reborn as their children. Giving trees and plants in charity pleases the gods. In the heat of the day, trees provide shade to weary passersby seeking some rest and respite. Droplets falling from trees after rains please our forefathers.

In the **Rig-Veda**, 6/48/17, it is said:
Do not be like the devilish buzzard that troubles other birds by catching their necks and killing them. Do not trouble the trees. Do not uproot or cut them. They provide protection to animals, birds and other living beings.

In the **Manusmriti** it is said that trees are like human beings and experience sorrow and happiness. God has created them for the welfare of living beings. They bring with them the fruits of their deeds from the last birth. They face the sun and the heat, but protect those who come under their shade. They provide refuge and an abode to birds and insects. They provide flowers and fruits. One cannot estimate the number of saints and sages who prayed under the shade of trees. It is a characteristic of trees to give, and keep giving. The Buddha is said to have attained salvation under a *bodhi* tree.

To Hindus the Peepal tree (the bo tree, *Ficus religiosa*) holds special significance. In the **Taittriya Sanhita**, the Peepal tree is included amongst seven most important trees in the world. The importance of the Peepal tree is also narrated in the **Brahmavaivarta Purana**. In the **Padma Purana**, it is said that the Peepal tree is a form of Vishnu, which is why Hindus revere it. Many describe it as a divine tree, as an object worthy of worship. Prayers are offered to it on several occasions around the year.

In the **Skand Purana**, Nagar, 247/41-44, it is said:
Vishnu resides in the roots of the Peepal tree. Keshav (a name for Krishna) resides in the trunk, Narayan in the branches, Sri Hari in the leaves and all the gods reside in the fruits. This tree is like the idol of Vishnu. All good people serve the virtues of this tree. This tree is full of all kinds of virtues and has the ability to fulfil desires and absolve sins of people.

Many Hindus believe that Brahma, Vishnu and Shiva reside in the Peepal tree. Hindu women believe that by offering prayers and watering the Peepal tree regularly, and by

circumambulating it, they will be blessed with good children, particularly a son. Souls that reside in the tree are pleased and enable the oblations to bear fruit. It is also customary to tie threads around the trunk of the tree. Pouring a little oil in the roots of the tree and lighting a lamp near it on Saturdays helps get rid of the malefic effect of the seven and half years of Shani. The shadow of Shani resides in the tree.

In the **Bhagavad Gita**, 10/26, Sri Krishna says:
Amongst trees, I am the Peepal tree.

The Peepal tree converts carbon dioxide into oxygen round the clock. Those who live nearby obtain more oxygen. It is noteworthy that during the summer, the shade of the tree is cool, but during winter, there is warmth in the shade. The leaves and the fruits of the tree are used for medicinal purposes. Devotees ensure that there is at least one Peepal tree within the precincts of a temple. The cutting or destroying of a Peepal tree has been equated with the murder of a Brahmin.

During *Vat Savitri* ladies pray to the *Bargad* (the Banyan tree — *Ficus indica*). Prayers are offered to the banana plant on Thursdays. The use of banana leaves for serving food is considered pure and clean. Prayers are offered to the Parijat tree (the queen of the night — *Nyctanthes arbortristis*; it is one of the five trees said to exist in paradise) as though it were the Kalpvriksha (the wishing tree obtained during *Samudramanthan*).

On Ashok *ashtmi*, prayers are offered to the Ashok tree (*Saraca indica*) to end sorrow and usher in hope. Special prayers are offered to the Amla tree (*Emblica officinalis*) during the Hindu month of *Kartik*. Vishnu visits the tree at that time. Ladies circumambulate the tree asking for a happy married life. The leaves of the Mango, its bark and the wood are used for a variety of prayers, ceremonies and yagyas.

In the **Brahmavaivarta Purana,** it is explained that in an earlier birth, Tulsi was Vrinda. She was married to an Asura named Jalandhar. To gain victory over Jalandhar,

Vishnu persuaded Vrinda to give up devotion to her husband. Pleased with her, Vishnu blessed her. She became Tulsi and is worshipped by people all over the world.

Most Hindus believe that there should be at least one Tulsi (*Ocimum sanctum*) plant in the courtyard of every home. In the **Skanda Purana,** it is written that one gets rid of the sins of as many lives as the number of Tulsi plants that one nurtures. In the **Padma Purana,** it is said that if there is a garden of Tulsi plants in the house, it becomes like a place of pilgrimage.

Prayers are offered to Tulsi especially in the Hindu month *Kartik* by growing new plants. The leaves of the Tulsi plant have excellent medicinal qualities. Whoever consumes Tulsi

leaves thrice daily achieves the purity and benefits of the *chandrayan fast*. Bathing with water that has a few leaves of Tulsi is likened to an important pilgrimage. Adding Tulsi leaves to the *charanamrit* offered in prayers helps get rid of sins. Even at the hour of death, it is customary to mix Tulsi with water from the Ganga and put it in the mouth of the dying person. This entitles the dying person to a place in Vaikunth.

From the scientific point of view, Tulsi is excellent for physical and mental health. It is known to cure serious ailments, as well as boost the immune system, vigour and vitality. It is extensively used in Ayurveda.

In most Hindu homes, prayers are offered to the Tulsi plant in the morning, and a lamp is lit beside it in the evening, before prayers. Thus do Vishnu and Sati Vrinda bless one. The penance of Vrinda, and her surrender and devotion to Vishnu are reflected in the fragrance and leaves of the Tulsi plant. It is customary to circumambulate the Tulsi plant 108 times on *Somvati Amavasya* (Monday that coincides with the dark night of the month).

In the **Brahmavaivarta Purana**, Prakritikhand, 21/40, it is said:
Bhagwan Sri Hari is not as much pleased after bathing with thousands of pots filled with the celestial nectar, as he is when even a single leaf of Tulsi is offered to him.

Flowers are dear to everyone. For Hindus, they carry a special significance. Flowers are offered to gods and goddesses when praying, fasting and conducting rituals and ceremonies. No ritual or ceremony is complete without them. The fragrance of flowers pleases the gods and goddesses. The beauty of flowers inspires us. They are a symbol of happiness and contentment.

In the **Sharda Tilak** it is said:
The forehead of a god must always be adorned with flowers.

In the **Vishnu Nardiye** and **Dharamottar Purana,** it is said:
Gods are never as satisfied with gold and gems, or with fasting or penance, as they are when flowers are offered to them.

In the **Lalita Sahasranama**, flowers strung together as garlands (*mala*) are praised thus:
A mala is an ornament. Of all kinds of malas offered to God, those made of lotus and pundreek (white lotus) are considered most auspicious.

In the **Ramayan,** the concern for plant life is evident when the physician Susena who treats Lakshman with the Sanjivini herb, asks Hanuman to restore the Dronagiri hill to its original location. The valuable herbs that grew on it could not survive for long in the new environment. Appreciating the point, Hanuman immediately restored the hill to its original location.

Hindus see divinity in flowers, in trees, shrubs and herbs. Every region has its own varieties of plant life. Flowers are flowers. They will give off their fragrance. They will win your heart through their splendour and multitude of colours. Devotees offer these in prayer at home and in the temples. When offered in prayer, they enhance the divinity of the gods and goddesses, giving eternal joy.

21

Divinity In Scriptures

DIVINITY IN HOLY SCRIPTURES

Ignorance is the root of all suffering. The only way to dispel ignorance is to counter it with knowledge. Many Hindus seek this knowledge through a guru. The vast majority, however, seek it from parents, the elders in the family, through rituals conducted within the family, and through a variety of books.

For a publisher, a bookseller or a librarian, books are the purpose of a business or service. Once a book finds its way to a Hindu devotee, who feels that the knowledge in the book leads to spiritual growth, it no longer remains an ordinary book. It begins to occupy a special position. It becomes a pathway to one's god or goddess.

For millions of Hindus, religious books and scriptures are a subject of reverence and worship. They are often kept protected in a cover, many times in a red cloth that is symbolic of auspiciousness. When reading the book it is often placed on a pedestal or a reading stand. Sometimes, little pillows support it.

Hindus attach great importance to the reading of religious books and scriptures. Whenever formal readings of the Ramayan, the Bhagavad Gita, Shiv Puran and other religious texts are done, a kalash filled with water and covered with a coconut tied in a red cloth is placed nearby. A lamp is lit for the duration of the reading. This is symbolic of the presence of Agni, the Fire God, and Varun, the Sea God. After the reading of the holy book, part of the water is consumed as though it were nectar, and part sprinkled in the house to usher in auspiciousness.

Like the holy books, the idols of the deities, the pictures, the rosary, the conch shell, or the bell, the lamp and the incense stand become symbols of divinity that lead the way to one's god or goddess, or both. The god or goddess of choice begins to reside within the prayer paraphernalia, and are accorded respect and reverence due to a deity. Most Hindus do not handle these items until after a bath, or at least after rinsing the hands well. Many feel that the touch of outsiders may defile them.

Most Hindu homes have a small personal temple or a corner reserved for prayers. A poor person would make do with only a picture of a god or goddess, perhaps cut from an old calendar or magazine. The family visualizes their god or goddess within the picture. To a devotee, anything that leads to a god or goddess is divine. It is a pathway to a higher, more sublime plane of existence.

22

Pleasing the Gods and Goddesses

PLEASING THE GODS AND GODDESSES

An important attribute of every god and goddess is benevolence: the ability to give freely. Many of the gods are benevolent almost to a fault. Some beneficiaries misuse their gifts, only to be set right later.

Every individual aspires for a share of this benevolence. The simplest way to please one's god or goddess is through prayer. For most Hindus, praying to God is a part of everyday life. It may just be a short thanksgiving to God, or a request for a favour. Some pray individually. Others pray in a group. There is no restriction on the choice of a god or goddess, or the mode of prayer. For every Hindu, it is a way of expressing one's faith and devotion to God. It is a way of connecting with a powerful force that has no equal. It helps to transform one into a better person. A little progress is achieved each day, and helps to cushion one from the buffets of everyday life.

In the **Mahabharat,** Anushasan Parv, 149/5-6, the importance of prayer is described as:

Whoever devotedly bows, pray and meditates shall be free from all problems through reverence and offerings to the omnipotent, omnipresent and omniscient God.

In the **Bhagavad Gita,** 9/26, Sri Krishna says:
The devotee who lovingly offers me flowers, fruits, food and other items is generous and wise. I accept the offerings as a token of love and symbolically eat them.

In the **Bhagavad Gita,** 18/46, Sri Krishna says:
Through one's good deeds and prayers to God, an individual finds divine contentment and salvation.

In the Hindu way of life, even children are introduced to prayer at an early age. Hindu rites, rituals and customs prepare them. Even Hindu festivals and fasts that are connected with gods and goddesses remind them of an individual's dependence upon them.

Many utter a specific prayer each time. They may have picked up the words from a religious book or discourse.

Some read prayers from a book or books dedicated to different gods. The most popular one is the *Chalisa,* a compilation of 40 verses in praise of a god or goddess. Some read the Bhagavad Gita, and others the Ramayan. Sikhs read Japji Sahib or the Guru Granth Sahib. Many prefer to choose their own words in prayer. Since a prayer is a personal communication with God, it may be worded in whatever way a person likes. The important thing is one must speak with sincerity. The words must come from the heart.

Group prayers are popular with many Hindus. Most of the groups are small, and the prayers are

conducted in the home or a temple. With many pandits reading the Ramayan, the Bhagavata Purana or other popular scriptures, gatherings become very large. The principal benefit of these occasions is the generation of positive vibrations that influence many people, for the good of humankind.

How and when individuals are transformed through religious experience is very difficult to say. Every individual is at a different stage of spiritual growth. Therefore, the influence on each individual is difficult to predict or assess. Once an individual begins to enjoy the experience, there is no telling where the person will reach. One develops a new kind of perception, is able to visualize life from a wider angle and shed false values that disillusion humankind.

Perhaps no other religion has as many kinds and occasions of fasts as do the Hindus. There are fasts for every day of the week. There are fasts that are observed once a fortnight or even once a month. While it would appear appropriate to feast on the occasion of birthdays of many gods like Shiva, Sri Ram or Sri Krishna, millions of Hindus celebrate them with a fast. Maun Vrata — a vow of silence — is another kind of fast.

Conducting a yagya with offerings to Agni, the Fire God, is popular in many Hindu homes. Special prayers on the occasion of Basant Panchmi, Shivratri, Ram Naumi, Ganga Dussehra,

Janmashtmi, Raksha Bandhan, Navratri, Dussehra and Diwali invoke the blessings of various gods and goddesses. A fortnight each year is devoted to remembering forefathers, who are no more with us.

As one connects with his or her god or goddess, the attention shifts to meditation and greater self-knowledge. Some may accept (indeed, frantically seek) a guru who can guide them to greater spiritual growth. Others follow the path of gaining knowledge through self-study and discussion with friends having a common aim. The company of good people is an important step for spiritual growth.

God created the universe. All living and non-living beings are the creation of God. What could be a better way to please the gods and goddesses than to serve those created by God? God created all living beings to serve each other. A cow provides milk not only for its calf, but also for humankind. A sheep provides wool just as the silkworm provides the fibre for silk. Trees provide shade and fruits to everyone. In contrast, man is selfish. He is ever ready to take from whoever is ready to give, but rarely shares what he has. When man sets out to serve, it means he is rising above his selfish nature, and moving towards the ideals set by God.

We have seen how the gods and goddesses have come down upon earth on many occasions to relieve the suffering of the common people. We have seen how we cannot survive without fresh air, water or the food the gods and goddesses provide. We may not be able to rise to become a god or goddess, however, we can surely rise above our selfish nature to serve the weak, the under-privileged and the downtrodden. In so doing, we would be repaying our debt for what we have received, and also achieve greater spiritual growth. Nothing would please the gods and goddesses more.

Epilogue

An individual is just a tiny speck in the vast cosmos created by the Supreme Being. His lifetime is not even a wink in the immeasurable eons that comprise cosmic time. The many gods and goddesses, too, are part of it. Creation is just one aspect of the Supreme Being: the balance maintained between the planets, the stars, and an unimaginable number of beings is the greatest miracle, which no one has been able to understand or explain.

A study of the Hindu gods and goddesses teaches us that the Supreme Being has not overlooked anything while creating and prescribing a way of life for all beings. In blessing us with life, the Supreme Being has accepted us as His children. Only we have abused His generosity, and misinterpreted His love and compassion. Through our own weaknesses, we have invited grief and suffering for ourselves.

As His children, He has given us all of His attributes. Rather than worship the gods He entrusted to look after us, we nurture the demons through our weaknesses like anger, hate, fear, greed, jealousy, attachment and lust. The study of the gods and goddesses teaches us that many before us did the same, but achieved nothing. They met an unhappy end. If we have understood this simple truth, we have truly learnt a great lesson.

Flowers are colourful, fragrant and attractive. They are dear to all gods and goddesses. In the **Padma Purana**, 5/84, the details of 'flowers' that gods and goddesses desire are given. Non-violence is the first flower, a control over the senses is the second, compassion is the third, forgiveness is the fourth, peacefulness is the fifth, control of the mind is the sixth, meditation is the seventh and truthfulness is the eighth. Gods and goddesses are pleased with a variety of flowers. However, none please them more than the inner peace and harmony of a devotee.

Individuals seeking the patronage of gods and goddesses are really in search of heaven, an abode of bliss. They fear hell. Hell is what one does not like to experience. It is pain and suffering that one fears. It is the fruit of actions, both good and bad. Hell is not a place. It is a situation that emerges from our negative thoughts. Heaven is the opposite of hell. It is an experience of joy and happiness. It comes from positive thoughts and actions. You experience it through your thoughts. Wherever you are, if you are at peace and harmony with yourself, you are in heaven.

In the **Bhagavad Gita**, 18/46, Sri Krishna says:
An individual finds divine contentment and salvation through good deeds and prayers.

The Supreme Being has created a perfect universe where He abides in everything. He has placed gods or goddesses everywhere, to ensure our welfare. Wherever we go, we are surrounded by His divinity. The truth is that both gods and demons are within us. Whom will we permit to take control?

HINDOOLOGY
BOOKS
An imprint of **Pustak Mahal**

FAIRS & FESTIVALS of INDIA

FAIRS & FESTIVALS OF INDIA

Unfolding the colourful cultural heritage of India

S.P. Sharma & Seema gupta • Size: 8.25"X10.5"   Pages:148 (H.B.)

Fully Illustrated in colour

Other books by **Pustak Mahal**

A clear and concise
account of Vedas,
Puranas, Upanishads
and Gita

J. M. Mehta
Size: 5.25" x 7.75"
Pages: 112

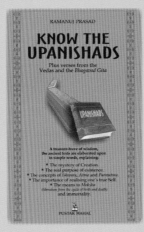

Ramanuj Prasad
Size: 5.5" x 8.5"
Pages: 120

Dr. Raj Kumar
Size: 5.5 x 8.5"
Pages: 136

Ramanuj Prasad
Size: 5.25" x 7.75"
Pages: 328

A Glimpse of the Sacred Himalayas

This book deals with the location, description, and significance of the places of religious and spiritual importance like Rishikesh, Haridwar, Panch Prayag, the Char Dhams namely, Kedarnath, Badrinath, Gangotri and Yamunotri, the Hemkund Saheb, the Valley of Flowers, Mata Vaishno Devi temple, Amarnath, Kailash and Mansarovar.

The Himalayas have lured people to this region since ancient times. References about the Himalayas are found even in the Rig Veda, the oldest scripture in the world. The Himalayas mean different things to different people. For sages, saints and seekers, it is a spiritual centre beyond comparison. Since time immemorial, ascetics have climbed the great heights in search of peace and wisdom.

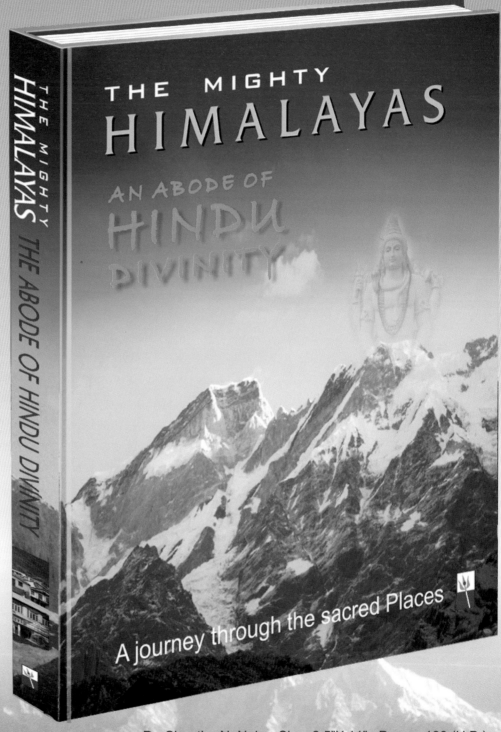

THE MIGHTY HIMALAYAS

AN ABODE OF HINDU DIVINITY

A journey through the sacred Places

Dr. Shantha N. Nair • Size: 8.5"X 11"   Pages: 100 (H.B.)
Fully Illustrated in colour